THE LIFE I SAW

SHARDA GULATI

For my grandchildren

Neil and Jay

Nikhil and Rahul

Lipika and Kashish

Contents

Preface *vii*

Acknowledgements *ix*

Prologue *xi*

1. My Childhood 1
2. My Mother : A Woman Ahead Of Her Time (1903 - October 1986) 14
3. My Brother Ravinder Kumar Sethi, A Sibling Like No Other 19
4. Anecdotes From Childhood 27
5. My Father : My Pride 32
6. Prison Diaries 38
7. The Riots And The Bloodbath Of Hatred 42
8. The Last Train From Sargodha To Amritsar 50
9. India My Country 56
10. My College Days 65
11. My Work : My Passion 69
12. A Match Made In Heaven 76
13. Our First Born 85
14. A Happening Life In Ambala (jan 1962 - Nov 18, 1971) 89
15. Punjabis Were Not Welcome In Rohtak (nov 1971-feb 1976) 105
16. Chandigarh - The City Beautiful 111
17. Family: My Most Valuable Asset 124

Contents

Thank You, Dear Mom! 133

Preface

I am neither a writer nor a poet. In my younger days, I used to write a diary in Hindi in which I would pen down my thoughts, interesting incidents of the day and inspirational quotes. Punjabi and Hindi have primarily been the means of communication (both written and verbal) in my personal and professional life. Though my medium of instruction during graduation and post-graduation was English, I am not very proficient in this language.

The journey of this autobiography, which is now in your hands started in 2017, about five years ago when I casually read out a few anecdotes from my diary to my daughters. My scribblings impressed my middle daughter Sujata, a writer herself, so much that she urged me to write my memoirs in English. I laughed it off. I have lived an ordinary life, there is nothing significant in my life which is worth documenting. To write in English was another handicap but every time we met, she would start off.

In 2018, my husband passed away and I came to Mysore to live with her for a few months. I had nothing much to fill my day, so I decided to write about my early life as a creative distraction. Sometimes I would struggle with the memories, and sometimes the thoughts would come but not the words. Nevertheless, I continued writing in bits and pieces whenever the mood struck. Simultaneously, I began reading English novels which helped in improving my expression and language. Gradually I started enjoying this exercise and looked forward to my day. Sujata's husband Rajiv too keenly listened to my narrations which was encouraging. Soon the dinner time discussions revolved around these stories where my son-in-law and both the grandsons participated enthusiastically.

This autobiography is an attempt to document my family's rich heritage. My father who fought for the independence of the country, was an epitome of compassion and selflessness. My mother was a woman ahead of her times. It's an honour for me to be their daughter. Unlike millions of others who perished in the mayhem during partition of India, my immediate family was fortunate not to have faced much hardship but it was a fresh start to our lives.

This work has reference to social conditions in pre-independence era, the migration, life at refugee camps, relocation, rehabilitation, and aftermath in post-independence era. In those times when girls were married off early, I did post-graduation in Political Science. I wanted to get married without dowry, and I got in-laws who firmly refused to accept anything other than the girl. Writing about my younger days was like reliving my life all over again; the faces which were long forgotten reappeared in front of my eyes, and I even connected with a few.

As I relive old memories and reminiscence the milestones in my life, the appreciation I received on many occasions during my life journey, I feel humbled as these commendations and accolades were due to the generosity of the people who were connected with me in many ways. I am fortunate to have met good people in my life who helped me grow personally and professionally. This autobiography is a tribute to those who made my life meaningful.

Acknowledgements

I am grateful to Sujata who has worked diligently to complete this work speedily to keep me alive through these memoirs, after I am gone. My cousins pitched in with their inputs. Gurmukh depicted the ordeal his parents went through during the riots, their dramatic escape from Khiali (Pakistan) to Sangrur (Punjab), and also about his father's struggles in restarting his life. Harcharan gave an account of his family's journey from Nankana Sahib (Pakistan) to Sangrur. Darshan narrated how his parents' small house in Sangrur became a place of refuge for the visiting relatives who came in droves from the other side of the border. It was heart-warming to listen to their stories. I thank my brother Ravi who tied the loose ends wherever needed with his memories. Equally commendable is the contribution of my sister-in-law Kusam who proofread the manuscript.

Prologue

Till I SEE the MIRROR

I am reminded of the episodes told by my mother
In spite of being the 3rd daughter in the family, I was loved by kith and kin
I was dark skinned but didn't have any inferiority complex
I am reminded of the episodes of my school days
Beaten by a classmate for breaking her inkpot in class two
Waiting till midnight for reciting a poem in a Jalsa or Gurpurab at Sargodha
Keeping the secret of failing in Stitching, History and Geography from my parents in class eighth
Gossiping with my classmate Madhu Kapila while sitting on back bench in class ninth
My ambition to be a doctor, which I could not be
Feeling like a young spirited girl with ambition to do something great in life

NOW WHEN I SEE the MIRROR

My total grey hair, toothless jaws, paining knees make me realize what a long path I have treaded
87 years, only 13 years less of a century
I feel, it is right time to reflect over the past and count my blessings

CHAPTER I

My Childhood

I was born on March 3, 1935 at Sargodha (now in Pakistan). I was third in the line of daughters in the family. My parents had their first offspring (my eldest sister Krishna) ten years after their marriage. Three years later, the second daughter Kamla arrived and then after about three years I was born. Ravi, my younger brother and now my only sibling was born three and a half years after me. Unfortunately both my sisters died young. Krishna, the eldest sister died of Typhoid at the age of fifteen, and the second sister Kamla died when she was six years old.

In those times, having three daughters was not less than a curse for parents. I was not only the third girl child but also dark complexioned unlike both my sisters who were fair. They were obviously beautiful and I wasn't because in our country beautiful means fair complexioned.

My life has been smooth and devoid of any drama but interestingly it started with a filmi drama – a drama so perfectly scripted by Ram Piara Lal, one of my father's very good friends. Fondly addressed as Chacha ji, Ram Piara Lal was an advocate by profession and the first person to be reached out in need. He had a son about the same age as Kamla. Incidentally when my mother was expecting me, his wife Dhanwanti (Chachi ji) was also expecting her second child, their dates of delivery just a day apart.

March 3, 1935, in the morning Chachi ji gave birth to her second son and the same evening my mother had her third daughter (me). Even before the babies were born, Chacha ji had a secret plan in his mind which he had not shared with anyone, the least of all with father with whom he shared everything. Chacha ji had held the news of his son's birth a secret from the neighbours and had instructed the Dai (mid-wife) to inform him as soon as the baby was born to my mother. As instructed, Dai ran to Ram Piara Lal's house to inform him about my birth. On learning that the third girl child had been born in his best friend's house, he knew it was the time to put his secret plan into action. He quickly wrapped his new-born son in a blanket and rushed to our house. Father was sitting in the baithak (drawing room); ignoring him, Chacha ji marched into the bedroom where mother was lying down on the cot with the new born (me) by her side. Without a word, he placed his son next to mother and carried me. Meanwhile father had walked to the room and was shocked to see the exchange of babies.

'Ram Piara! What's happening?' He was confused.

'Shh...,' Ram Piara Lal said, putting a finger on his lips. 'No one yet knows about the birth of these babies. I already have a son and you've two daughters. You take my son and I take your daughter and tomorrow we'll declare to everyone accordingly,' he whispered.

Father laughed taking me back from his friend, 'I highly appreciate your sacrifice but it doesn't matter to me if I've a son or a daughter. Both are equal.'

'But, I thought...'

'No but, and now take your son back to his mother.'

When I think of Ram Piara Lal, I wonder how could anyone sacrifice his most beloved possession for the sake of a friend. Now a days, before doing even the smallest favour, we think of our benefit in the bargain.

I take pride in being the daughter of a true humanitarian who sacrificed his life for his country. He passed away at the age of 51. I was only 15 at that time. I have tried to retain the values I imbibed from him. He didn't have a long life but it was a fulfilling one, spent for the good of humanity. As Abraham Lincoln said, 'And in the end, it's not the years in your life that count. It's the life in your years.'

Today as I sit down to write my memoirs, I celebrate his life.

In earlier days the date of birth of girls was not recorded. Interestingly I calculated my own date of birth while submitting the examination form for my matriculation exam. I was told by mother that when I was about three months old, a massive earthquake occurred in Quetta (Pakistan). I found out, on May 31, 1935 a powerful earthquake devastated the town of Quetta and the adjoining areas which killed nearly 35,000 people. Another clue which came in handy in the calculation of my date of birth was that I was born in the midnight of 18th and 19th in the month of Phalgun which was the month of February/March as per Indian calendar. On the basis of these calculations, I wrote my date of birth as March 3, 1935.

Because the parents didn't note down the date of birth of their girl child, the girls never got to celebrate their birthdays unlike their brothers whose date and time of birth was duly recorded, and horoscopes were made for them. I remember, on my brother's birthday every year, mother prepared prasad and took it to the gurdwara.

I wasn't fair complexioned like my sisters

I was told I was a cheerful baby. I would gurgle and smile at everyone who peeped into my cradle. One day father asked mother the reason for my cheerfulness. Mother replied, 'being the third daughter and also dark complexioned, she is aware that she is not going to get any attention so she tries to attract people through her smiles and gurgles.'

As the years passed, gurgles turned into giggles and smiles into laughter. The giggles and laughter continued as I grew up and started going to school. Every day after school I would stop by a family friend's house. They had seven daughters, none of them were even close to my age but I loved visiting them. Of the seven sisters, I was fondest of Shanta, the eldest daughter. Incidentally she was also dark complexioned like me. Shanta must be around eighteen years at that time and I was seven; she would make me sit on her feet and swing me enticing giggles from me.

One day she asked me playfully, '*Sharda tu meinu eni changi kyon lagni hein?*' (Why do I like you so much?)

'*Behenji, tuwada mera rang iko jiah hae isi karke.* (Sister, you and I have the same complexion. That's why)

The entire living room burst into laughter.

Most people in Punjab are fair complexioned and even as a child I was aware that I looked different. I longed to be fair and beautiful. I had a friend named Indu who had a peaches and cream complexion. At night I would sleep with a prayer on my lips that when I wake up in the morning, May God turn me into a fair skinned girl like Indu!

As I recall these incidents, I realize I must had been conscious of my dark complexion. Interestingly, even though I wished I were fair complexioned like other girls, I didn't have any inferiority complex. I never considered myself lesser than others because of the colour of my skin. I never hesitated to make new friends, meet people, take initiatives, deliver lectures on stage and even at the time of my marriage, the colour of my skin was never the cause of any insecurity within me. The colour of my skin was one of my physical features. That's it.

My School days

My early schooling was in Sargodha. I studied at Arya Girls School. Sanatam Dharam and Khalsa school were other good schools in the city with equally huge buildings and large playgrounds. None of the schools those days were co-educational. My school was a ten minute walk from home. I would get ready and walk to the school, kicking the dust with my shoes on the way.

The school started at 9 a.m. and ended at 3 p.m. Each class had twenty five students. There were no benches or chairs in the class, the students sat on the jute mats. The teachers were addressed as Behen ji (sister). The primary school children used takhti (a rectangular wooden plank) and Qalam (reed pen made from bamboo) to write. Pen/ pencil and paper were introduced only in the middle school. The tip of qalam was dipped in the liquid black ink to write on the takhti. After writing, the takthi was left to dry for a few minutes. Back home takthi was wiped clean with gachani (multani mitti/fuller's earth) to make it ready for use again. The ink available in tablet/powder form was mixed in water to prepare the liquid ink which was then poured in a small pot of glass or metal for everyday use. Most children used metal inkpots because they were easier to handle. Glass inkpots were expensive and considered to be classy.

Sheela, one of my classmates had a beautiful glass inkpot. Once I accidently broke her inkpot. Sheela was furious when she saw her inkpot lying broken on the floor, tiny glass pieces strewn around, splashes of ink all over the floor and on my clothes. She whacked me for breaking her inkpot and demanded money as a compensation for her loss which might be a fraction of a paisa. I am not sure if I'd cried but I was dead scared of the beatings so I promised to give her the money. I used to get one dhela (half a paisa) everyday as my pocket money which I usually spent on eating papad or something spicy from the vendors outside the school. From next day onwards I started giving her my entire pocket money as a compensation for her broken inkpot. I did that for many days. In addition to monetary compensation, she would beat me up. Irrespective of how much money I paid to her, it was never enough like a sahukar's (money lender) debt. I continued to pay her in cash and kind. When the beatings didn't stop and I couldn't take it any longer, I started avoiding going to school. I would make an excuse of stomach ache or headache. I hadn't yet told about it to mother but she observed that I was reluctant to go to school. One day she followed me to the school. The moment I reached the school, Sheela whacked me. From a distance mother saw me getting beaten by a girl and understood the matter. She met the teacher who scolded Sheela and rescued me from her clutches.

I wore knee-length frock with churidar to school and elsewhere. There was no uniform in schools. Except father's shirts and pyjamas (which were stitched by tailor), mother stitched clothes for all of us. The fabric was bought in bulk and stitched whenever needed. Mother was fond of her Singer sewing machine which was brought to India along with the rest of the luggage during migration. Purchased a few months before my birth, this machine remained with mother for whole of her life, and was discarded much later. Father's clothes were sent to the laundry for washing and ironing whereas the rest of the clothes were washed and ironed at home with a coal iron.

Home sweet home:

Street name: Block 14
City: Sargodha
Country: Undivided India
Block 14 was a narrow street with single-storey houses on either side. The houses were joined together by a common wall between them. Ours was a rented house at a monthly rent of Rs 15. The house had two entrances – one entrance was to the living room for the formal guests to enter. The second entrance opened into the cemented front yard which led to the three rooms. The room on the extreme right was used to keep fodder for the buffalo, the middle room was the bedroom and the room on the left was the store.

The rooms were big and had minimal furniture. There were no cupboards in any of the rooms. The clothes were kept in iron trunks. The quilts and blankets which every household had in plenty, were stored in large iron trunks, and the daily wear clothes and woollens went in smaller trunks. At the end of the winter season, the woollens were aired in the sun and packed in trunks with naphthalene balls and dried Neem leaves to save them from pests.

The middle room, which was the bedroom for the family had a large cot and a couple of trunks. The cot was knitted with colourful cotton tape and had multicoloured legs. At night, we pulled extra charpais into the bedroom for everyone to sleep. In summers, because it was hot we slept on the rooftop. In case it rained at night, we would fold our mattresses and rush down. There were ceiling fans in both the drawing room and the bedroom but in peak summer even fan couldn't provide any relief. The ceiling fan in the drawing room was of Crompton make which we carried with us when we migrated; it was disposed of much later. There were electric bulbs in all the rooms but we also used kerosene lamp to go to the darker corners of the house which were not well lit.

The kitchen was at the end of the covered veranda outside the rooms. Sitting on a low wooden stool, food was cooked on earthen chulha (U shaped mud stove made from local clay) using cow dung cakes and wood as fuel. The bathroom which was open to the sky was to the left of the front door. The toilet without any roof and door was on the rooftop. It might be unimaginable for the present generation that there was no flush system. Every morning, the sweeper collected the excreta in a basket, washed the toilet, and left carrying the nightsoil on the head.

The flooring in the house was of red bricks joined together with cement. Because there was not much furniture in the house, the floor was washed every other day. Water supplied by the municipality was available all the time. There was no separate water supply for drinking, the same water was used for drinking, washing and cleaning. We also had a handpump in the bathroom. In summers water from the handpump was cold and in winters the water that came out after pumping for a few minutes, was lukewarm.

The common wall between our house and the adjacent house to the left had a brick size hole which was big enough for a bowl or a plate filled with savouries to pass and also for the women to chit - chat while they went about their day in the front yard.

The family that eats together stays together

Parathas (potato, radish, cauliflower, fenugreek) eaten with curd and mango pickle, is the staple food in every home in Punjab. The breakfast has always been a variety of parathas. I don't know any Punjabi who is bored of eating parathas all seven days of the week. Lunch consisted of a seasonal vegetable, curd and roti. Popular vegetables were potato, beans, okra, carrot, bitter guard, bottle gourd, pumpkin, radish, turnip, yam, sweet potato, and a variety of greens. I had never heard of capsicum. Tomatoes which were first planted by the British were sparsely used. Dinner was mostly dal and roti. We didn't eat much of rice. The food was cooked in home-made pure ghee.

Sargodha was a hub of citrus fruits. Besides the citrus fruits like oranges, malta, mithas, there was a wide variety of seasonal fruits available such as mangoes, musk melon, watermelon, falsa, pear, and sarda (a type of musk melon). In summers mother roasted rotis on the earthen tandoor. Besides rotis, the tandoor was also used for roasting round brinjals for making bhartha. Placed in the front yard, the tandoor was about three feet tall. Cotton wood / thicker stems of cotton plant were used to generate fire in the tandoor. In summers women from the neighbourhood got together and roasted rotis on a tandoor in anyone's house. This time was best used to catch up with the neighbourhood gossip. On most days mother made extra rotis to give to a beggar or an animal.

Mother was an excellent cook. Besides the delicious meals she cooked every day, she was equally adept in preparing sweets and savouries such as besan ki barfi, mathis, mesu, shakkarpara, karachi halwa. Besan ki barfi was mother's speciality. The snacks and munchies were stored in the large ten litre tin boxes (tinplate containers). When the contents of the box were about to be over, she would sit down again to make those mouth-watering delicacies whose taste lingered in the mouth long after consuming them. Rice kheer, halwa, custard and firni were the other desserts she prepared very well. The two most popular desserts during those days were kheer and wheat flour halwa.

We also had a kulfi making hand machine at home whose exteriors were like a wooden bucket. The inside aluminium container was used for the ingredients. Crushed ice was put around the aluminium container and later salt was sprinkled on the ice to prevent it from melting. Churning ice with the handle resulted in freezing of the milk leading to formation of kulfi from milk. It took about half an hour to churn one litre milk.

Purchasing confectionery items over the counter was not really the trend though there were a few confectionery shops in town. I remember accompanying mother to one of the bakeries to get the biscuits baked. We would carry the ingredients such as wheat flour, milk, ghee, sugar and salt to the bakery and in an hour return home with a tin full of freshly baked biscuits and khatai whose aroma wafted through the entire house.

It was common for the well-to-do families to own cows or buffaloes. We always had a buffalo instead of a cow because mother liked thick milk. During the day, the animal was tied outside the house and in the evening she was brought inside and tied in the foyer. She gave about ten litres milk daily which was consumed by the family in the form of milk, curd, buttermilk, butter, ghee, and paneer. The leftover buttermilk was given to the neighbours, the helpers who came to work in the house or the workers in the neighbourhood. Because there were no refrigerators, the milk had to be boiled multiple times in a day to prevent it from curdling.

In the morning mother would sit in the veranda to churn out butter with madhani(wooden hand blender). Some was consumed during the day and the leftover butter was collected in a big container and stored in the jallidaar cupboard (cupboard with mesh doors). When the container was full, mother made ghee out of it. Once when she was pouring ghee in a large iron tin, she noticed something black and long in the container. My nani (maternal grandmother) was around, she stretched her palm and mother put that black and long thing on it. When mother and nani were looking curiously and imagining what it could be, a woman from the neighbourhood walked in. 'It's a snake. Throw it away,' the woman cried. The snake was already burnt and dead.

Now the question was what to do with the ghee. The ladies didn't have the heart to throw about ten ser (approx. ten litres/kg) ghee down the drain. A suggestion came which they approved instantly. Use the ghee to make washing soap. Caustic soda and oil are two important ingredients for soap-making. Caustic soda is poisonous; if two poisonous things are combined, they kill each other's poison. It was decided to use the ghee (poisoned by the presence of snake in it) as a substitute for oil to make the washing soap. The idea was excellent but mother could not rely on anybody. What if the man sells the ghee! It could endanger the lives of gullible buyers.

After much effort, a professional soap maker was summoned to make the soap in our house. By evening, the entire year's supply of washing soap was ready. After an year, the man was summoned again and this process was repeated as mother had found a dead rat in the tin of ghee. We again had the washing soap supply for another year.

A few of the many fond memories from my childhood are of our family outings to the cinema hall. Whenever my parents had some free time, we went to watch a film. Sargodha had a single cinema hall with a seating capacity of about three hundred – two hundred in the lower class and hundred in the balcony. Besides lower class and balcony, there were two box cabins for VIPs. I remember watching the film Devdas in the theatre. Father was a well-known person and was offered the box cabin for his family to enjoy the movie in privacy but he always insisted on buying the tickets and sitting in the balcony like other people. He didn't want any special treatment for himself and his family.

I couldn't make much sense of the movies still I enjoyed going to the cinema hall, it was a rare family outing. I loved dancing and singing though I believe I have two left feet and I am only a bathroom singer. I was intrigued by how actors perform from behind a curtain. Every time I watched a movie, I wondered why we can't do the same at home. 'Why don't we demolish the wall of a room and place the curtain there and we can ourselves sing and dance? *Fiv cinema ban jayega hov tavan da. Hov tavan da.* (It'll be a different type of cinema) I danced and sang repeatedly. Till the age of seven, I pronounced R as V.

One of the memories from the school days is of an RSS camp held at our school premises where self-defence training was imparted to girls. During the two-week duration of the camp, we were put up in the school and taught how to use lathi (stick). I was in 7th standard at that time. During the training, we were made to stand in the line according to our heights. Being the shortest and the youngest, I was always the last one in the line.

I had no stage fright

Because I emulated my father and I had seen him speaking at functions, I always looked for opportunities to speak on the stage. Famous Punjabi poet Ram Lubhayamal Tayyar, who was a friend of father, would write poems for me to recite at public functions and gurdwaras.

Those days the winds of patriotism had started blowing swiftly so most of the poems the poets wrote were about patriotism and love for one's country. Women empowerment was the other subject on which people spoke in public gatherings. It was in these sabhas that I had my baby steps in public speaking. Sometimes the sabhas and gathering would go on till late evening but I would patiently wait for my turn and would go home only after reciting the poem. In case it got late, mother would leave early, requesting one of the neighbours to drop me home after my performance.

CHAPTER II

My Mother : A woman ahead of her time (1903 - October 1986)

My mother Mohan Devi Sethi (maiden name Kesran Devi) was born in Khiali village about 3 km from Gujranwala. She was a pampered child as many of her younger sisters and brothers had died, and she remained the only child for quite a long time.

How mother learnt to read and write

Mother was a quick learner and curious about learning new things. Education in her times was the rarest of the rare commodity in villages not to speak of girls but also for boys. People who valued education sent their sons to schools in nearby towns but this opportunity was denied to girls. My maternal grandparents Charan Das and Dhan Devi were progressive thinkers and wanted their daughter to be literate but there were no schools for girls. Nana ji had a shop where items of daily use, groceries, fabrics etc were sold. He was literate in Gurmukhi (Punjabi) and Urdu. He could read Guru Granth Sahib and recite shabads. He was also fond of teaching.

In the evenings after returning from the shop, he would teach Gurmukhi to the girls of the neighbourhood. The teaching would happen in one of the three rooms on the first floor of their big house. Till late evening, he would be surrounded by little girls enthusiastic to learn how to read and write, a couple of kerosene lamps lighting the room. There was no electricity in the village. Nana ji often told mother to join the class but she wasn't interested. Playing outside was more fun. Veeran, mother's close friend was a regular to the class but mother had no motivation to learn.

One morning, mother and Veeran were returning home after taking bath in the village pond as they did every day. There was no water supply in the village houses and people defecated in the fields, and bathed in the ponds. After bath Veeran started reciting Japji Sahib path. Unaware, mother continued talking.

'Kesran, don't disturb me, I'm reciting Path,' Veeran scolded mother.

Mother glared at Veeran. How dare she talk to her rudely? It's only because of her father that Veeran can recite Path. Without saying a word, mother ran off leaving Veeran. At home, she complained to her father. 'How can she ask me to shut up? It's only because of you that she can read.'

Nana ji listened to her patiently and when she was done, he replied calmly. 'If you also learn to recite Path, one day you can give her tit for tat.'

This was a trigger enough for mother to start her journey towards literacy but she wanted to do it secretly, not sure what the reason was. Either she didn't want her parents to know that her friend's taunt had triggered the change in her or she wanted to show her worth only after she had learnt something. From the next day, mother set on her literacy journey.

One day when nana ji was taking out a post card to write a letter to an uncle, mother offered to write for him. He laughed, 'Will you write? Do you even know how to write?' Nani ji asked nana ji to give mother a post card, and to let her scribble on it. Postcard was given and mother wrote as dictated. Though there were grammatical and spelling errors, the letter conveyed the message. For her parents it was unbelievable but true that their daughter knew how to read and write, so mother dragged them to the rooftop. The walls of the terrace were scribbled with alphabets in Gurmukhi. In amazement and delight, they stood there gazing at the blackened walls with charcoal. It was on these walls mother had practiced writing.

After mother had gained enough confidence she decided to read Guru Granth Sahib in the gurdwara. One morning she asked nani ji to prepare kada prasad (wheat flour halwa) for her Charni Lagna ceremony. In Sikh religion, to sit before the holy granth for the first time is called Charni Lagna. Nani ji rebuked her, 'You go and play, reading Guru Granth Sahib is not a child's play.'

It's a dishonour to the Guru if a person sits down to read the holy book and can't do it properly. Disappointed, mother went to her father's shop and asked her chacha ji (father's younger brother) who was manning the shop at that time, to give her some batashas (a sweet candy most commonly used as prasad in temples) to be taken as prasad to the Gurdwara. Her Chacha ji also chided her sending her away. Not to be discouraged, evading his eyes, mother sneaked into the shop, grabbed a handful of batashas from a gunny bag, hid them in her dupatta and ran off.

At the Gurdwara, bowing her head before Darbar Sahib, she placed the batashas in the container for keeping prasad and sat before the holy book for her Charni Lagna ceremony. Family was stunned when a village woman informed them that she had seen Kesran reading Guru Granth Sahib in the Gurdwara.

My mother's siblings, her pillars of strength

Mother was the eldest of four siblings. She had two younger brothers (Sant Singh and Preetam Singh) and a sister (Vidya) who was twelve years younger to mother. After their father passed away, Sant Singh, the older brother managed their father's shop along with their chacha ji who was already working with their father. Chacha ji never married and lived with the family for his entire life. Sant Singh and his wife Kulwant Kaur were of immense support to mother during Ravi's illness. Kulwant Kaur mami ji was a rare spirited person. Ravi was very attached to her, he wanted her to be around him all the time. Feeding, bathing, changing, everything had to be done by her. He insisted that only she fed him and put him to sleep. At night mami ji could hardly sleep because she had to get up quite a few times to change Ravi's soiled clothes. The diapers were not heard of in those times. In the morning, mami ji would carry the bundle of soiled clothes to the village stream to wash them. Many times mother offered to wash the clothes but mami ji wouldn't let her.

Sant Singh and Kulwant Kaur had four children (Sons Gurmukh Singh Jolly and Ranbir Singh, and daughters Jagdeesh Kaur and Sukhjeet Kaur who was born after partition).

The younger brother Preetam Singh was in the government service. He and his wife Basant Kaur had five children (Sons Harcharan Singh, Harbhagat Singh, and daughters Harjeet Kaur, Ranjeet Kaur (Guddi), Malvinder Kaur (Baby/Motia).

Vidya masi (her name was changed to Satwant Kaur after marriage) was married to Sardar Harwand Singh Chawla who originally belonged to Sargodha but lived in Sangrur in Punjab. He started his career in 1933 as a PA to the chief minister of erstwhile Jind state. In 1962, he retired as a superintendent of Punjab civil secretariat. They had six children. (sons – Harjeet Singh, Uttam Singh, Attar Singh, Sudershan Singh (Darshan), Upkar Singh, and daughter Jagdeesh Kaur).

We frequently met Sant Singh mama ji's family but couldn't meet other relatives often as Preetam Singh mama ji had a transferable job, and Vidya masi lived in Sangrur which was an overnight journey from Sargodha.

Mother at Ludhiana in 1976 with her two favourite accessories - her wrist watch and purse

CHAPTER III

My brother Ravinder Kumar Sethi, a sibling like no other

Ravi was born after much praying. After having three daughters, my parents were keen to have a son. One winter morning, a beggar came to our door. 'I don't want food, just give me some warm clothes,' he pleaded when mother went out to give him a couple of leftover rotis. 'May God bless you with a son!' the beggar said.

Inside father was getting ready to go to his hospital. He was dressed in a long woollen coat over khadi kurta pyjama, and white turban. Father heard the beggar, took off his coat and gave it to him. Not sure if this act of kindness was done out of sympathy for the beggar who didn't have warm clothes or for the blessings. Father was generous and always helped others.

Mother (addressed as Mata ji) was a devout Sikh. Once on Panchami day she went to Chheharta Sahib gurdwara near Amritsar to pray for a son. It was believed that a dip in the sacred sarovar could fulfil your every wish. After taking a dip in the sarovar, she took a vow that if she was blessed with a son, she would visit the gurdwara on twelve Panchamis (need not be consecutive). Panchami comes once in a month. It was an overnight journey by train from Sargodha to Amritsar so she was practical enough not to make a false promise even to God that she would visit the gurdwara on consecutive panchamis. An year later, on September 7, 1938, a son was born to my parents.

After Ravi's birth, mother kept her vow and visited

Chheharta Sahib gurdwara on panchamis. The eleven trips were made without any hiccups. In early 1944, that day we set off for the twelfth and the final time. Father was in Mianwali jail for his participation in the Quit India movement. Elder sister Krishna had passed away. After praying in the gurdwara, mother went to take a dip in the sacred sarovar while nani and I stayed outside trying to mind Ravi who was about five years old and very mischievous. Mata ji had just come out from the sacred sarovar when Ravi ran towards her and clung to her legs, not letting her move.

'Go away. Are your legs joined together that you can't stand straight?' She shrugged him off. This was the same spot where she had prayed for his birth. Mother bit her lips the moment the words escaped her mouth; it was not her habit to abuse or curse anyone, the least of all her children but the curse had already had its impact perhaps.

Contented that her vow was complete, we left for the railway station and boarded the train from Amritsar to Gujranwala (a big city and district H.Q) for the return journey. From Gujranwala we would take tonga to reach our native village Khiali which was about 3 km away. The next morning when we were gathering our things to get off the train, Ravi's shoes were missing. Little did we know that it was ominous. It wasn't anything to be worried of, they were just an old pair of shoes, someone in the train might have flicked them off. It happened all the time in trains. Before hiring the tonga to our village, we went to the market to buy a new pair of shoes for Ravi. Khiali was a small village and had no footwear shops. At the shop, Ravi happily put on the brand new shoes but when he was asked to walk to check if the shoes were comfortable, he just couldn't walk. Mother tried her best but she couldn't persuade him to walk. We went to the village assuming he must be tired or just adamant but next morning he again refused to keep his feet down on the ground. A week passed and he still couldn't walk. The family panicked.

Immediately the word was sent to father in the jail. In no time the doctors started visiting us from far off places to examine Ravi. Medicines, injections, ointments were tried but all in vain. By now mother had lost her sleep. Someone suggested taking him to Buddhagraya village where a man named Labh Singh could cure anyone. Labh Singh was believed to be the descendent of Bhai Lalo (disciple of Guru Nanak) and had a unique God-given gift. There were strange stories about patients going to him on someone's shoulders and coming back walking. Mother was a modern woman, she didn't pay any heed to such irrational beliefs. Moreover the road to Buddhagraya village which was about 15 km from Khiali, was kaccha and the horse/mare was the only means of transport. It wasn't easy to carry a five years old child that far.

One morning mother was upstairs when her eyes fell on a young boy in the opposite house. The boy was afflicted with polio and was walking on his fours. Her head zoomed, she imagined her own son walking on his fours. Something came to her mind, her hands reached for Ravi who was sitting nearby. Plucking the child in one swift move, she ran down, calling out for her sister-in-law (Kulwant Kaur mami ji). 'I'm going to Buddhagraya , tell Sant Singh (Mama ji) to come if he wants to,' she said and left.

Mami ji wrapped the leftover rotis from the previous night and some mango pickle in a cloth and rushed to inform her husband who was milking cows in haveli nearby where the family kept their pet animals. Mama ji immediately took out his mare (wealthy people used mares as a mode of private transport), and followed his sister to Buddhagraya village.

Miracles do happen

It took them about nine hours to reach Buddhagraya. The brother sister took turns sitting on the mare and carrying the child who was cranky and restless. Labh Singh, the magic man, lived in a hut whose entrance was so low that one had to bend down to enter. Exhausted from the day long journey, mother put Ravi down on the charpai and sat on the floor in a heap. Labh Singh was not at home at that time. Though no one informed him, he had got an intuition that a patient was waiting for him in his hut. He walked in, 'Behen(sister), you've only one son, so many people told you to come but you've taken so long,' he said to mother.

Surprised that he knew it all, mother looked at the man pleadingly and said, 'Bhai (brother), now that I've come, do whatever you can.'

'I don't have any herbs today, come some other day,' he said flatly.

They were disappointed that the child couldn't be treated that day but grateful that he hadn't turned them away. 'We'll come some other day but do something now so that we reach home comfortably,' mother pleaded. He assured them that they would reach home comfortably.

Since morning no one had eaten anything and Ravi had been lying listlessly without a morsel in his stomach. On their return journey, he demanded food. The packet of rotis was immediately opened. When he asked for water, they stopped at a well, mother took off her dupatta and mama ji his turban and together they dipped it in the well, drew it out and squeezed the water in Ravi's mouth. Unlike their previous journey which had taken them nine hours, their return journey was quick. By evening they were home.

After a week, Mama ji went back to Buddhagraya to bring the herbal medicines prescribed for a week. The recovery was quick and within a month Ravi was walking, running, jumping and yapping. When Ravi had fully recovered, Mama ji paid a visit to the miracle man to thank him. 'What should I offer you as a gratitude for what you've done for us?' Mama ji bowed his head in front of the noble man.

'What business do you do?' Labh Singh asked.

'I've a cloth depot.'

'Then get me a turban, this one is torn,' the miracle man said pointing towards the torn turban on his head.

I wouldn't hesitate to add if this anecdote was narrated to me by someone else, I wouldn't have believed it but when something like this happens in your own family, in front of your own eyes, you have to believe that miracles do happen. I wonder where have the miracle men gone? Why miracles don't happen now?

In 1948, we went to Chheharta Sahib gurdwara again to thank the almighty for his blessings, this time taking a bus from Jalandhar to Amritsar. By then the country had got freedom and we had relocated to the new land which is called Bharat.

Ravi is younger to me by three and a half years. His nick name is Minna and mine Cheecho, so people used to call us Cheecho Minna. Both of us went to different schools as there were no co-educational schools. Our schools were close by so we would leave and return home together. We used to quarrel a lot with each other. He would grab my hair from the crown and pull them hard. I have always had long hair, and when anyone complimented me, he would proudly say that he had made them long by pulling every day. Except the few hours that we spent in our respective schools, we were inseparable.

When father was in jail, mother did all the chores herself because we couldn't afford a helper. She would wake up early, have her bath and go to the gurdwara at 4.30. On return from the gurdwara she would churn milk, cook, clean the house and wash clothes. In the evening, when she went to the gurdwara again, Minna and I washed the utensils, I cleaned the brass utensils with rakh (coal ash) and Ravi rinsed them.

An interesting episode of our affection for each other is still fresh in my mind. A few lanes from our house lived a Bedi family comprising four brothers. Their parents had passed away long ago. Only the eldest brother was married. The two older brothers were from the clan of freedom fighters like father which perhaps was one of the reasons that our families were close.

In 1945, it was the marriage of the second eldest brother. Since the brothers didn't have a sister, they wanted me to accompany the baraat (groom's wedding procession) for the Vagh Fadai ceremony. (A ceremony where the sister ties the hair of mare with sacred thread). The marriage was to take place in Lahore. I didn't want to go without Ravi but neither Bedis wanted to take him nor mother wanted to send him. He was only seven and I was about ten - not grown enough to take care of a child.

The following day the baraat was to leave for Lahore at 6 a.m. so the Bedi brothers took me to their house the previous night. I wanted Ravi to cry and make some noise so the family would be compelled to take him too but sadly he didn't create a scene. The entire night I couldn't sleep because I hated to go with the baraat without my brother. In the morning, when I woke up, I ran home. It was summer and Ravi was still sleeping on the roof, mother was downstairs. As soon as I entered the house, I started calling Ravi's name loudly, as loudly as my lungs would allow. Minna... Minna... I wanted him to wake up so that he would insist on coming along with me but mother scolded me asking me to keep quiet. Meanwhile two Bedi brothers had arrived home looking for me. They had panicked when they didn't find me on the bed. They carried me back to their house and then to the bus for Lahore.

For two days when I was away from home, I missed Ravi all the time, didn't enjoy the festivities at the wedding, didn't relish the sweets. I was waiting for the wedding celebrations to be over so that I could go back to be with my brother. I wished he were with me so that he could also enjoy the celebrations. Every time anything was served I saved a little for him.

After two days the wedding party reached back Sargodha. It was early morning when the bus arrived. I alighted from the bus, picked up my bag and ran home where my Minna was waiting for me with lots of eatables which mother had cooked in my absence. He didn't want to eat them without me. During the last two days he hadn't gone to school. '*Shada bina dil nahi karda.* (I don't feel like doing anything without Sharda),' he said repeatedly in my absence.

When I reached the marriageable age, Minna used to tell me not to get married so that both of us could be together forever but mother advised me not to listen to him. She said when he is of right age, he would get married and have his own family. By then I would've crossed the marriageable age and would have to live the rest of my life taking care of his kids.

We didn't let the love and affection between us subside on growing up. I sincerely wish all siblings are close not only in their childhood but also when they are adults. Even now when we both are in our eighties, we debate, argue and even disagree on matters but we are just a phone call away from each other. I also shared excellent relations with his late wife Surya who was an ideal daughter-in-law to my mother and a loving mother to Ravi's son Deepak.

CHAPTER IV

Anecdotes from Childhood

Most of my childhood memories are from my mother's maternal house in Khiali as all my summer vacations were spent there.A Muslim family lived in the adjacent house. They had three daughters and two sons. I was friendly with one of their daughters named Bilkees who was about my age. When I visited our native village, Bilkees and I would sit in her house through the nights singing songs and playing but I never ate in her house as eating and drinking in a lower caste or Muslim household was a taboo. Once while returning from the village, I asked Bilkees to write me a letter so that we could stay in touch. She was shocked as if I had committed a crime. Letter writing by girls was considered to be a sign of bad character.

My sisters

I have absolutely no memory of my second elder sister Kamla who passed away at the age of six. I was three years old at that time but I do remember my eldest sister Krishna who was six years older than me and very authoritative. Our nani to whom we addressed as Bebe was very protective of her. In the evening, a male tutor used to come home to teach Krishna who was about fifteen years old, and was studying in class tenth. When the tutor was home, Bebe made sure that she stayed around in the room.

It was the summer of 1944 when Krishna got typhoid. She recovered after three weeks but soon had a relapse. In those days, relapse of typhoid always turned out to be fatal. In spite of the treatment her condition worsened day by day. Because father was in jail, the menfolk from the neighbourhood would visit us every morning to inquire if the family needed anything. At night they took turns to stay with us. For the entire duration of her illness, every night Krishna would have bouts of high fever. To bring down the fever, a cloth soaked in ice water was kept on her forehead. For this purpose, slabs of ice were bought from the ice factory, and kept wrapped in big jute sheets to prevent it from melting. One night the fever was exceptionally high. It appeared Krishna's end was near. The word spread. More neighbours gathered.It was midnight when her condition worsened. Krishna was on the cot in the front yard, her eyes closed. Mother sat by her side pressing her arms and hands.

Krishna half opened her eyes and looked at mother, 'Mata ji, may I go?' she asked, her voice faint.

Mother thought since her daughter is destined to leave this world why block her way. 'Yes dear you may go,' she said bravely.

'Mata ji, with whom should I go?' Krishna opened her mouth again.

'Putar, Ramchander ji and Sita ji have come to take you in their viman (aeroplane/vehicle), you go with them.'

'Achcha (Okay),' Krishna said and folded her hands in namaste to the people standing around her charpai with moist eyes. She brought her hands down and again lifted them. 'My deep regards to my father, the king of Sargodha,' she said, closing her eyes.

Her funeral was attended by each and every person of Sargodha.

Even animals can sense danger

Mother was fond of travelling. In those times, people travelled either to visit relatives or for pilgrimage. Mother loved both. There were many gurdwaras around Amritsar. Whenever we went to Amritsar, we booked a room in Guru Ramdas serai at Golden temple, and went around visiting nearby gurdwaras during the day and would be back to the serai in the evening. Next morning we would go again. Buses and tongas were the two main means of transport. Buses had no fixed departure time. Whenever a bus was full, it would start off. Tongas were a preferable mode of transportation for short distance travel as they were readily available.

On one such sojourn, we were going to a gurdwara in a tonga. Bebe and mother were in the back seat with Ravi in mother's lap, and Krishna and I were on the front seat next to the tongawalla. I was carrying an aluminium container with a handle which we filled with guavas. The tongawalla was a kind man and the horse was obedient so the journey was smooth. When we were only half way through, the tongawalla stopped for a while to take rest. The animal too needed a break. He said he was tired and would ask his brother who lived nearby to take us on the onward journey. Soon, the brother arrived. The moment mother set eyes on his brother, her intuition alerted her that he was not a decent man. She didn't want to go with the new tongawalla but she had no choice.

The second leg of our journey started. We had travelled only a short distance when the horse stopped. The tongawalla whipped the animal but it refused to budge. Not only us but even the animal had sensed the evil intentions of the tongawalla. The tongawalla saw me biting into a guava and yelled asking me to give the fruit to him which startled us.

'Beta, give it to your mama ji,' mother asked me. She addressed him as brother so that he wouldn't harm us. Even mother calling him as her brother didn't improve his behaviour. Mother didn't show but she was petrified, a lone tonga wading on a deserted road with a young mother, an elderly grandmother, two young girls and a toddler but she didn't let her face reveal her nervousness. The tongawalla continued whipping the animal but it refused to move. Left with no other option, tongawalla about turned the tonga and voila, the animal literally ran. When the tonga reached the same spot where the drivers were changed, he handed the reins to the old driver. Surprisingly, the animal showed no resistance now and the rest of the journey was completed without any trouble.

Do animals sense danger? Perhaps yes.

Hindu Water Muslim Water

Hindus and Muslims were two different religious communities. It was a fact accepted and respected by both. Marriages between these two communities were unthinkable. Not just the matrimonial alliance, no Hindu ate or drank in a Muslim household though they visited each other's houses and attended weddings and celebrations. In our home, there were separate vessels for father's Muslim friends and other Muslim visitors. This differential treatment didn't offend anyone, it was taken as a norm. I remember during our train journeys there were vendors on the station who offered free drinking water. The platform would be abuzz with the calls of Hindu water... Muslim water... by the vendors.

We had a young Muslim boy named Alia who milked our buffalo. Alia would come in the morning, give bath to the animal, feed her, milk her and then tie her outside the house before leaving. In the evening he would come again to milk the animal and then would tie her back inside. Most households gave food to their helpers besides the salary. A ceramic plate and a bronze glass were kept separately for Alia. After having rotis and lassi, he would wash his utensils, keep them separately and leave.

On our travels we carried rotis whose dough was prepared with milk and not water because it was believed that anything cooked with water can be contaminated by the touch of a person outside your own caste but anything cooked with milk cannot, perhaps that was the reason the buffalo's milk was not contaminated by the touch of a Muslim boy. As Hindus didn't eat at Muslim weddings and other celebrations, Muslim households would send ingredients generally used for making sweets (such as shakkarpara, mathri, laddoos etc called *suki bhajji* in Punjabi), to their Hindu friends so that it could be prepared at home. In spite of Hindus not eating in Muslim households and keeping separate vessels for their Muslim friends at home, there was communal harmony between the two religions.

CHAPTER V

My father : My pride

My father Dr Lehna Singh Sethi (1899 - Dec 1, 1950)was born in a middle class Sikh family in village Dadan near Gujranwala. He had four siblings - three brothers and a sister. His father Sunder Singh Sethi had a small shop and his mother Moola Devi managed the house. My paternal grandfather (Dada ji) died of plague when father was 5 years old. At that time father's eldest brother Barkat Singh was twelve years old, Ishwar Singh, the second eldest was eight. Father was the middle child. Shyam Singh, the brother younger to father was two and a half years, and the new born sister (Kartar Devi) was eight days old. After dada ji's demise, dadi ji moved in with her maternal family. Dadi ji was not in perfect health and couldn't look after her children.

Dadi ji's sister-in-law (brother's wife) took care of the house and the children including her own. Dada ji was a Sikh and all the four sons had long hair as is the practice in Sikh religion. It was quite a task for the sister-in-law to maintain the boys' hair - clean, wash, comb and tie them in a joora (bun). One day a barber was summoned, and father and Shyam Singh were given a haircut. The two elder brothers were spared because they were not at home when the barber came. As a result the two elder brothers remained Sikh and the younger ones became Hindus. Earlier, Hindus and Sikhs were considered to be a single community. The men who wore long hair and beard were called Kesadhari and those without beard and long hair were called Sahejdhari.

Marriages were common between the two communities. Dada ji was a Kesadhari Sikh whereas dadi ji's maternal family was Sahejdhari Sikh. Kartar Devi, the sister was married to a Sahejdhari.

When the brothers grew up, the eldest brother Barkat Singh opened Sethi Shoe Shop at Block 10 in Sargodha. He was married to Durga Devi. They had eight children (Five sons - Avtar Singh, Jagdeesh Kumar, Balkrishan, Rajkumar, Sukhdev, and three daughters - Kaushalya, Sumitra, Dmanyanti. Barkat Singh died when he was in his early 40s. Ishwar Singh, the second brother died when he was in his twenties and still unmarried. Shyam Singh, the younger brother was married to Rampiyari. They had a son and a daughter named Krishan and Krishna respectively. Sister Kartar Devi got married to Amarnath Chhabra who hailed from Sialkot. They had two sons – Ramesh and Brij. I don't remember much of my dadi ji as she mostly stayed with her younger son Shyam Singh at Basti in UP. We lived in Sargodha. Dadi ji was too frail to travel so she hardly visited us.

Father's education, a stroke of luck

The village where father lived had no school so the boys played in the fields all day. Once father and his younger brother were playing in the field with other children. A British soldier was passing by on a mare. The boys found a distraction and started pelting stones at the mare which obviously infuriated the soldier. Immediately he went to the village sarpanch and complained about the boys' mischievous act. Sarpanch was a reasonable man, he calmed the soldier down and said, 'because there is no school in the village, the children have nothing to do except play and trouble the passers-by.' The soldier informed his superiors and within a month, their village had a school. Father, Shyam Singh chacha ji and a few other boys were enrolled in the first batch.

After a few years, the school was closed for lack of students but by then father and his brother had passed the middle school. Since the boys were already studying in a school, the family didn't want them to discontinue their education. They were enrolled in a high school in a nearby town. Father studied up to class ten, found himself a job, later took medical education and became a medical practitioner. His brother Shyam Singh did BSc and went on to become the Chief Chemist at Basti Sugar mill in Basti. Father was a great believer in destiny, he always said the school was opened in the village just to lead him and his brother on the path of education.

Father was nineteen years old when he got married. He worked in a shop at a monthly salary of thirty rupees. Mother was fifteen at that time. A few years later he happened to meet a close friend Dr. Pindi Das who became furious when he learnt about father's salary. 'How do you manage in such a small salary with a widowed mother and a wife,' Pindi Das reprimanded father, and advised him to take admission in a medical college and become a doctor like him. When father thought carefully, he understood the truth in his friend's words. Thirty rupees was too low a salary to take care of a family of three. The next day he boarded the train to Agra and enrolled himself in King George medical college. It was a four-year course and education was free. The only condition was that after completing the course the students had to join the army. For that period,mother moved to her parents' place and dadi ji went to live with her younger son Shyam Singh in Basti. Father used to visit mother at Khiali during his holidays. In 1929, my eldest sister Krishna was born.

In the final year, once father accompanied a friend to a *jyotishi* (an astrologer). He asked the astrologer if he would pass the exam. The *jyotishi* read his palm and declared that he would fail. Father was disheartened. He put his books away. As he was not going to pass, why waste time on studies. After a few days father had a dream that he had failed in the exam. He woke up with a start and found himself sweating profusely. The dream shook him. If the dream of failure could shake him what would happen if he fails in real life. Only a few days were left for the exam. However better sense prevailed and father picked up his books again. He burnt midnight oil and passed the final exam.

In the same year, another life changing event happened. Father had an opportunity to listen to Mahatma Gandhi at a sabha. Mahatma's words inspired him so much that he decided to join the freedom movement. In March 1930, he completed his medical education and got the degree of LMP (Licensed Medical Practitioner). He was offered commission in the army with a fat salary and attractive perks but father already had his heart set on the freedom movement. When he refused the job offer in the army, his principal, an English man asked him, 'how would you manage your home if you deny this job?'

Father said he would open a clinic in his village. 'I'll treat people and they will give me a part of their produce. That'll be sufficient to feed my family,' he said. His confidence impressed the principal;he gave his blessings to father and asked him to follow his heart.

Those doctors who didn't join the British army had to reimburse the full amount of the fee to the college. Father's family was middle class and didn't have much money but it was out of question to join the British ranks. Mother's jewellery was sold to reimburse the fee to the college.

His participation in the freedom movement gave him a sense of worth as a patriotic citizen of the country but not money to run a household. To keep the kitchen fires burning, he set up a two-room hospital in Block 10 of Sargodha and soon became one of the most reputed doctors of the city. He was not only a good doctor but also a kind man. He charged a small amount of fee but the treatment to the poor was free. Later whenever he was in jail, the hospital was run by his two compounders. The hospital was closed down when father was imprisoned for three consecutive years for his participation in the Quit India movement.

Ravi and I with Father at Bradlaugh Hall, Lahore in 1945 after his appointment as the MLA of Punjab of Undivided India

CHAPTER VI

Prison diaries

Out of the seventeen years that father participated in the freedom movement, thirteen were spent in jail though not consecutively. Courting arrest for the freedom of the country was as much an honour for the family as for the freedom fighter. Those who couldn't take part in the freedom struggle due to whatever reasons too had a deep regard for the freedom fighters and their families. The Britishers arrested people at random. Anyone associated with the freedom movement even in a small way could be arrested anytime. The freedom fighters didn't resist the arrest but sometimes their followers insisted on the time and place of their choice.

Once a police party landed at our house to arrest father. People gathered outside in thousands. Public decided to dodge the police and allow father's arrest only at the gurdwara which was a kilometre away. The police party was at the door and it wasn't possible to take father to the gurdwara so people took him to the rooftop, and jumped through the rooftops of houses carrying him on their shoulders to reach the gurdwara where he courted arrest. Many horrifying thoughts must be running in mother's mind at that time. How many months he would be in jail, would he get enough to fill his stomach, would he be tortured, but like always she didn't let her face reveal her fears. Perhaps the women of the freedom fighters were as brave as the freedom fighters themselves.

During the Quit India movement (1942-1945), father was kept in jails of Punjab such as Multan, Sialkot and Mianwali along with other freedom fighters. In 1944 when he was in jail, sister Krishna passed away. He was allowed to attend the funeral only on the condition that henceforth he would shun the freedom movement but that was not acceptable to him. So he couldn't bid farewell to his first-born and see his daughter one last time. He was released after an year.

Prisoners were divided in three categories on the basis of their importance and crime they had committed. Prominent freedom fighters were A category prisoners and not considered as criminals. Father was an A category prisoner and we were even allowed to visit him in jail. Irrespective of their status, all prisoners were tortured. On one occasion father was made to lie down on an anthill during a hot summer day, and later beaten but he preferred to die for the freedom of the country than shift his loyalty. A number of prisoners who could not bear the torture, sought forgiveness from the British and gave an undertaking to never participate in the freedom movement. They were freed.

In jail, to pass his time, father wrote, read and spun cotton on Gandhi charkha. He spun a khes (cotton blanket) which was brought to India along with our other belongings. Father (addressed as Pita ji) always wore khadi. He wanted mother to follow suit but Mata ji wore it only on some formal occasions as she found the fabric rough. Like father, Ravi and I wore only khadi. Till my marriage, I didn't wear any other fabric. The saree I wore at my wedding was a khadi saree in pink with gota patti (a type of lace made from metal) stitched on it by mother. Before independence mill-made fabrics such as silk, plush, lathha, voile, satin, paplin, crepe, and other handmade fabrics like mulmul were also available but these were not within the reach of everybody for all time wear.Khadi being hand-spun and hand-woven was much cheaper as it was spun in almost every household. Later, on the call of Mahatma Gandhi, khadi became glorified as a symbol of patriotism.

It was common for the authorities to conduct raids at the residences of the freedom fighters. No warrant was needed to conduct the raid. When father was lodged in Multan jail, once a police party came home to conduct the raid. Mother was alone at home. Since there was no male member at home, she sent word for Pandit ji, our immediate neighbour. While mother stood outside, Pandit ji oversaw the raid inside as the police party of four led by Subedar went around the house tapping at iron trunks, earthen pots, looking inside the brass tumblers, feeling the sacks of fodder. 'It's my duty,' the subedar said apologetically for the nth time. Within minutes, the police party was out. Many times the raids were an eyewash as the loyalty of the police party (all Indians) was torn between their countrymen and the Britishers.

Sword of honour

In 1945 father was appointed as the MLA of Punjab of undivided India. After his swearing-in-ceremony, he visited the Golden temple in Amritsar where he was honoured with a sword.

Father at the rooftop of our house in Sargodha just before his arrest for his involvment in the Quit India movement in 1942

CHAPTER VII

The riots and the bloodbath of hatred

When the announcement about Independence and consequent partition of the country into India and Pakistan was made, not many thought about its implications. Some shifted to India by airplanes and trains for a short period carrying only a few of their belongings, certain that they would come back soon when things settled down.

Father was appointed Liaison officer to evacuate Hindus from Sargodha and the surrounding areas, and send them safely to India. He was offered a salary of Rs 800 per month but he refused to accept any remuneration for his work. He said until now he was in jail and couldn't do much for the countrymen, now was his opportunity to serve people. His service would not be a service in the true sense if he accepted money for it. He was already an MLA (Member Legislative Assembly) in Punjab and received a monthly salary of Rs 200 which he said was enough to take care of his family's expenses.

Migration from both sides of the border started. Like many, father too thought this to be a temporary phase but soon the riots started in Punjab, Bengal and many other states bringing home the realization that people would have to move immediately. Every day military persons would go with the convoy of trucks to the villages to evacuate the villagers and put them in camps in Sargodha until arrangements were made to send them across the border. Father and a few social workers would accompany the convoys in jeeps. The movement of people on the border had picked up pace. Hindus and Muslims who until now had lived in complete harmony became each other's worst enemies.It is difficult to tell if the leaders had expected such a bloodshed or if there were ways to have a smooth transition or if any political party was flaming it but once the carnage started, it was unstoppable and turned out to be the worst bloodshed. It was the biggest movement of people in the history of mankind.

In most of Punjab, there was death and destruction. The houses were burned and looted. The rioters dragged people out of their houses, killed men and children, and raped or abducted their women. The trains carrying refugees between the two nations would arrive with corpses, their passengers killed en route. They were called blood trains. The soil had soaked so much of blood that the fruits on the trees seemed to have the taste of blood. The abducted women were raped or killed. Those women who managed to escape their abductors were forced to live a life of hell because their own families wouldn't accept them. On one of the evacuation operations, a Hindu teenage girl was evacuated from a village. Her parents were killed by the rioters, her elder sister was abducted and the younger sister was missing. She was too shattered to stay alone in a camp.With nowhere else to go she was given shelter in our house. She stayed with us for more than a month. Later she was sent to some relatives in Jalandhar.

Sargodha Block 14, where we lived, was a Hindu dominated area with the exception of a few Muslim households in the back lane. During the riots, two daughters of a Hindu family used to sleep in our house at night. No riots took place in Sargodha and surrounding areas. The only casualty was four elderly men who were hacked by some miscreants during their morning walk.

Once the carnage started, each day mattered

The authorities on both sides of the border tried to make this transition a smooth affair. Father issued the passes to the residents of Sargodha to cross the border by train. The number of passes varied each day depending on the capacity in the train. Early in the morning, people would start gathering in the aangan (front yard) of our house, the queues spilling over on the road. Sitting on the diwan, father would be surrounded by people. Everyone wanted a pass at the earliest, each one's plead more urgent than the others. Widows and children were the first in the priority list. Some women would fake as widows to get the travel pass on priority. When there were more stories of bloodshed in the neighbouring areas, people panicked, their wails filling the house. Father would stand on the diwan and tell people to recite*Tera Bhana Meetha Lage* (The will of God is sweet and acceptable). He would tell them they had always recited this sholok in good times but now is the time they shouldn't forget its meaning. Father took a vow that his own family would be the last to leave Sargodha after every single person had left. 'And they would leave in the same manner as others,' he said. Despite having government paraphernalia at his beck and call, he didn't want any special treatment for his family.

Evacuation from my native village Khiali

In April 1947, mother's younger brother Preetam Singh was posted in Andaman, a place notorious for cellular jail (also known as Kala pani) where political prisoners were kept and tortured. Being a high level government official he had sensed that the migration of the population from one part of the country to the other would become imminent with the declaration of partition. He along with his wife and children came to Khiali to take out his mother and brother's family safely to Delhi. Nana ji had passed away long ago. Two days after he reached Khiali, he fell ill with typhoid. He was taken to Gujranwala for treatment but he couldn't be saved. A few weeks later he passed away. His wife Basant Kaur shifted to her maternal home in Nankana Sahib with their children.

In September 1947, Sant Singh's family would often see big fires in Gujranwala city from their roof top which worried them. A few days later they learnt about a couple of trucks parked outside the village. They panicked thinking the army had come to capture and kill them. The Hindu and Sikh families rushed to hide in Muslim houses in the neighbourhood. Sant Singh mama ji's family hid themselves in Amena Bibi's house. The truckers came to the village, searched for Hindu and Sikh families but couldn't find anyone.

After a few days the trucks came again but had to return empty handed as the non-Muslim families had gone into hiding. The street where Sant Singh mama ji lived had a dead end whereas the other end had a huge iron gate so the street was like a fortress even though the gate was never closed. One evening there was a call from the Muslim community asking non-Muslims to convert to Islam or get killed. That night mama ji locked the gate thus forbidding anyone to enter their street. At night a bunch of men from some other village came, shouting out slogans against Hindus and tried breaking the gate but thankfully they couldn't succeed. The goons left saying they would come again the following day with appropriate tools to break the gate. The entire night the family prayed to God, certain that they would be killed the next day.

The following morning the convoy of trucks came again. They saw an eighty-year-old woman outside a house who told the truckers that the Hindus and Sikhs were hiding in their houses. They were not rioters but military trucks especially sent for them by Kulwant Kaur's brother-in-law to evacuate them. Harbans Singh, husband of mami ji's sister had sent the trucks for the third time sure that if his sister-in-law's family would have gotten out of the village they would have come to them but they were surprised when every time the trucks reported that there weren't any Hindus in the village. The military evacuated the Hindus and Sikhs including nani ji, Sant Singh mama ji and his family. Sant Singh's wife was nine months pregnant. The evacuees were asked to carry their clothes,sacks of rice and black grams if they had at home which could be used for the refugees in the camp.

Sant Singh had a cloth depot. He also used to lend money to villagers for a small interest by keeping their jewellery as security deposit for the loan. When the villagers came to know that the moneylender's family was leaving, they rushed to take back their jewellery. Immediately the jewellery was given back but they refused to return the money they had borrowed. There was no time to fight over this, the trucks were waiting.

Sant Singh had hidden his wife's jewellery in a wall of the house for safe keeping. Sant Singh removed the bricks, took out the jewellery, wrapped it in a cloth and asked a trusted Muslim friend to hold it for him while he packed his luggage. The friend stayed around till the trucks left, hugged Sant Singh and handed him the packet in which the jewellery was wrapped. The friends bid goodbyes to each other with moist eyes. Later when Sant Singh opened the packet. It was only the cloth. The 'trusted' friend had betrayed him. Mother's chacha ji who lived with them, didn't want to leave the village. He ran away to the fields and hid himself there. It took the family an hour to find him. They picked him and put him in the truck.

The family was put up in a camp in a gurdwara in Gujranwala. Here a baby boy was born to Kulwant Kaur mami ji. Bebe somehow managed to reach home through the deserted woods to pick up some clothes and vessels. Unfortunately within a few days, the new-born died in the camp.

Later the evacuated families were taken to Lahore and finally to Amritsar. On the way to Amritsar the convoy of trucks carrying them stopped on the GT road for an hour. One of their neighbours' eldest son Amrik Singh, a handsome newly married man got down in search of water but he didn't come back. He was killed by Muslim hooligans.

The family reached Amritsar penniless and homeless. In Pakistan, they had lived in a big house, owned properties, had a flourishing business. Here in the new land, they had to start their life from scratch. How difficult it is for anyone to start afresh in the middle age but there was no choice. Sant Singh had a family to feed. He bought a sack of sugar, sat on the road side and sold the sugar. He made some money and bought another sack to sell. When he had enough money to buy train tickets for his family, he took a train to Sangrur where his sister (Vidya masi) lived.

Later in Sangrur he found a house abandoned by a Muslim family, and occupied it. Meanwhile his brother Preetam Singh's wife and children who had also migrated to India from Nankana Sahib with some relatives, had reached Sangrur. They too found an abandoned house and settled there. Sant Singh borrowed Rs 300 from mother to start business. Once his business established, he returned the money to mother.

Vidya masi's house - a refuge for relatives

After partition, masi's house in Sangrur gave refuge to a large number of relatives including her brothers' families, her husband's relatives, and old neighbours from Khiali who migrated to India in droves and were homeless. When the numbers swelled, and masi's small house couldn't accommodate so many people, a haveli nearby was taken on rent. People slept and bathed in that haveli but they all ate at masi's house. At times there were close to fifty people eating in their house. Ration was bought on credit.

During the day the men would go around the city looking for work or an abandoned house to live permanently. The hosting family didn't have deep pockets but they certainly had a big heart to provide shelter to so many people. Gradually the relatives found their feet and left.

After migration when we shifted to Jalandhar, then to Ludhiana and finally settled in Jalandhar; I met my entire maternal family often and grew closer to all my cousins. After my marriage, when masi's family was stationed at Ropar and I was in Ambala, I would visit them on my way back from official travels. In 1977 after masi's husband passed away, and the three elder sons migrated to the US and Canada, she continued to live with her son Darshan in Mohali (near Chandigarh). The youngest son Upkar Singh also lived there. She lived up to 99 and passed away in 2012 at Darshan's house.

Vidya masi with Gurmukh Singh Jolly (Sant Singh mama ji's eldest son) in the US in 1983

CHAPTER VIII

The last train from Sargodha to Amritsar

November 1947. It was almost the end of November when everyone in Sargodha city had been evacuated safely and it was the turn of our family to leave. The days had become shorter and air had turned nippy. Mother, Ravi and myself were put up in the last train from Sargodha to Amritsar. Father was to join us later after completing all the evacuation related formalities. Our luggage was a pitcher of water, three bedrolls, and two iron trunks containing father's medical books and a few clothes. Father came to see us off at the station and arranged our luggage in the coach, the bedrolls in front of the windows to work as shields in case the bullets were fired from outside, the trunks went under the seats.It was November and the orange crop had yet not ripened but the farmers had plucked the unripe oranges to sell to the departing people and make some profit. Father bought a couple of dozen oranges for us to quench our thirst in case the water in the pitcher got over. He took all precautions for our safety but there was no fear in his eyes.

Besides mother, Ravi and I, the other people travelling with us were Hardevi bua and Saraswati bua (our two elderly neighbours to whom father considered as sisters and I called them bua), Gian Chand Sethi chacha ji (a close family friend) and Avinashi Bhappa (our neighbour Pandit ji's eldest son to whom I addressed as bhappa - elder brother). Soon the train chugged out of Sargodha railway station. The coach was full, people had occupied every inch of space available inside the coach and also the roof. When the train reached Lahore railway station, instead of going towards Amritsar, it started moving backwards towards Badami Bagh station. People started crying fearing they would meet the same fate as some previous trains from which the passengers were pulled out of the trains and killed with swords and knives. All one could hear was shrieks and cries of people. Abruptly the hue and cry stopped. An announcement over the public address system was being made - 'A refugee camp has been arranged at DAV College Lahore. Leave immediately, the trucks are waiting outside the station to ferry people to the camp.'

The passengers jumped off the stationary train carrying whatever luggage their hands could hold. In hurry, our pitcher of water fell down and broke. There was no porter to carry the luggage to the waiting trucks which were parked at a distance from the station. It was impossible to walk with our entire luggage. Mother emptied the trunks of books and kept only the clothes and other essentials. The others who were with us had to carry their own luggage so there was no one to help us with the luggage.

Ravi and I carried a few light things and walked towards the trucks. Mother came slowly carrying heavier objects. When the trucks were full, one by one they started leaving. Mother hadn't yet reached. We started crying. A young Sikh man standing nearby asked Hardevi bua ji why we were crying.She told him about father and also that our mother was still at the station. He ran after the moving trucks and brought back the last one. Meanwhile, mother arrived, and we all boarded the truck.

Refugee camp at DAV College Lahore

'Refugees' was the new name given to the Hindus arriving from Pakistan. DAV college turned into a transit camp for the refugees who were reaching by trains or kafilas. From here, they would be sent to Amritsar by trucks. Tents were erected in the college grounds. At any given time, there were a couple of thousand people in the camp, their number swelling by the hour. People kept their belongings under their rugs and slept on it to save it from the bandits. The fear was not just from the rioters but also from other refugees. Even if we were stationed in the premises of a college, the fear of being killed lurked everywhere.

For the first two days we slept in the open as all tents were full. On the third day a tent was allotted to our group. We were eight of us in a 12 by 12 ft tent. Sajjan Singh (the young man who'd stopped the trucks for us) had tagged along with us as he was alone. He seemed to be a kind man so no one objected. Gian Chand Sethi chacha ji and Avinashi Bhappa were of immense help throughout the journey. Gian Chand Sethi had already sent his wife and children to India with his elder brother but he had stayed back to accompany us.

As Gian Chand Sethi had the same surname as ours', father considered him as his brother. His wife Rampiari belonged to father's village so she was like a niece to father; we addressed her as Behen ji, and she called my parents Chacha ji and Chachi ji. I can never forget their support to us when father was in jail. They ran errands for mother, and would come home every evening to inquire about our studies, Gian Chand chacha ji tapping his feet outside the door to announce their arrival. Similarly Pandit ji's entire family had left by a previous train. In the days of deadly violence and riots, it was a great sacrifice by their families who let them stay back behind to help us.

The Camp

People cooked food on the earthen chullahs in front of their tents. Some cooked at common chullahs taking turns to cook. Ration was provided by the camp authorities but it wasn't free. The temporary lavatories of the same material as the tents were situated at the far end of the ground, away from the tents but the old and sick who could not walk, eased themselves and defecated inside or in front of their tents. The air was foul all around resulting into many people falling sick.

Today's generation who enjoys separate bathrooms attached to their exclusive bedrooms cannot imagine the plight of people who were forced to defecate where they slept or ate. Dead bodies laid in the centre of the tent, relatives mourning and at the same time cooking, and eating - life went on. Many people managed to reach the camp safely but died due to hunger or disease.The last rites of the dead were performed by the volunteers and camp authorities. Our group was lucky enough to have survived the ordeal of the camp life.

One morning, Sajjan Singh went out and bought about a dozen Mithaas (a citrus fruit of orange family). Emptying the dirty cloth in which he had carried the fruit in front of mother, he asked her to distribute it amongst the people in the tent.

Mother was furious. 'Have you gone crazy? You're wasting money on this useless stuff, we don't know how long we've to stay like this? Just take it away.'

Giving her a glare, Sajjan Singh carried the mithaas and threw them out from the boundary wall of the college. Within minutes he returned, throwing his head at mother's feet, he cried, 'Mata ji, you've saved us. Mata ji you've saved us!'

The fruits had been injected with cyanide. Those who had consumed the fruit were dead.

From Lahore refugee camp to Amritsar

After one week, we were sent to Amritsar by bus, and put up in Makhdoom Pura, a Muslim dominated area now vacant as all Muslim families had fled. Makhdoom Pura was again a transit camp but had better living conditions. Here our original group got disintegrated. Sajjan Singh left. Avinashi too left to join his family in Ludhiana. Gian Chand Sethi chacha ji's family met us here and stayed with us.

Now instead of a tent, we were given a room. It was a 9 feet by 9 feet room for nine-ten people which was barely enough to keep our luggage. Our trunks, bags and bedrolls stacked one above the other till the ceiling laid against the walls. The space in the centre was used for sitting and sleeping. At night the men and boys slept outside while the women put their children on laps and drowsed. There was barely any space to stretch legs but even that claustrophobic room was a blessing. At least we had a roof over us and we were safe.

After five days in Amritsar we moved to Jalandhar where we were housed in Congress Bhawan in Pucca Bagh. At that time, father was the president of the Congress party in Punjab. Our family was given a two-bedroom set with a living room, independent kitchen and bathroom on the first floor. Gian Chand Sethi's family was given a room just across the narrow corridor. Two buas got a room on the ground floor. Father came to meet us whenever he visited India on official work but he finally joined us in September 1948. Father brought along with him some of our household goods including mother's sewing machine, a couple of paintings, a wooden trunk, two ceiling fans, some utensils and a few other items. Congress Bhawan was our residence and father's office for about two years.

A month after we shifted to Congress Bhawan, once an eight-nine year old boy about the same age as Ravi knocked at our door. He said his entire family had perished in the riots, and he was homeless. Mother brought him inside, gave him food and Ravi's clothes to wear. Because Chander was an orphan, and had no place to go, he lived with us. He was a friendly child. Ravi and Chander played together, when he went out to play wearing Ravi's clothes, they looked like real brothers. Chander would tell people that he was Dr Sethi's son. Chander also informed us that his father was a rich man and used to wear English style hat. Two months later, his family was found. They were not dead as told by Chander. He belonged to a poor family, and had run away from home in frustration. He was sent back to his family.

CHAPTER IX

India My Country

Congress Bhawan Jalandhar was our new residence in free India. The life which was in pause mode picked up again. Home, cooking, schooling started, it was a blessing to have come alive out of that ordeal. We didn't have to face the hardships faced by many other refugees. Except for a few days in the camp, where we had to sleep under tents and manage with little food, we always had a roof over us and sufficient to fill our stomachs.

When we left Pakistan, I was studying in 8th. In Jalandhar, I was again enrolled in 8th in a government school. Though I'd always enjoyed going to school, I was not academically inclined. Besides the compulsory subjects, there were a few optional subjects such as tailoring and embroidery for girls. The tailoring exam had two parts – homework and practical. For the practical part, the students were evaluated for the needle work done in the examination hall and for the homework, they had to prepare a design at home and show it to the examiner on the day of the exam.

Stitching and embroidery never interested me and I hadn't prepared anything for the exam, so mother gave me an embroidered tablecloth to show in the exam for which I was delighted. The white table cloth with red and pink embroidery was made by my sister Krishna for her 8th exam.

I must mention that mother never forced me to learn cooking or stitching, she always said the household work can be learnt at any age but not academic education. I carried the beautiful tablecloth with Sindhi stitch marks to the school and produced in the exam. The teacher inspected the intricate embroidery and turned towards her colleague, 'this looks like from that Punjab side.' (Most regions used to have embroidery and stiches specific to that area. Now-a-days because of internet, people have access to art from any part of the world but those days only if you have lived in that place, you would know the art forms of that region). This question was not addressed to me but I on my own said, 'yes it's from that Punjab side.'

They looked at me. 'Who made this?' they asked, laughing.

'It was embroidered by my elder sister for her 8th exam,' I replied innocently.

Sadly, no marks were given to me for speaking the truth. I got a big F in the subject, not just because of speaking the truth but also because I had done nothing in the practical exam which carried 75 marks out of 100. Not just the optional subjects, I had also failed in compulsory subjects like History and Geography. The end result was, I failed in 8th. I was scared to reveal the truth to my parents. I lied that my teacher had not promoted me to 9th class because I had flunked in the optional subject. Father was busy anyway and had no time to go to my school to check my results. I couldn't continue in that school because the government schools didn't promote the failures so I got myself admitted in 9th in a private school named Sai Das Girls School. Private schools admitted dropouts in the next class. Unlike today when the quality of government school education is much below the average standard, those days the government schools imparted a high standard of education.

The only memory from Sai Das Girls School is of my friend Madhu Kapila who was my classmate in 9th - short, wheatish complexioned and very talkative. She regularly attended RSS Shakha. After the session, she would narrate the teachings of RSS to me, one of which impressed me the most was to be respectful to everyone including the house maids. After one year when I shifted to Ludhiana and left that school, we lost touch.

In 1976 we reconnected in Chandigarh, when once I went with my husband to his friend Ramesh Kapila's house in Sector 23. A woman peeped from the glass window. Even before the door opened, I told my husband I knew this woman. He was surprised, how would I know his friend's wife. I had never met them. When the door opened and we were ushered in, I asked the friend's wife if she was from Sai Das School Jalandhar and if her name was Madhu. Life is full of happy coincidences. After that we met frequently. Madhu Kapila passed away in December 2021 in Chandigarh.

Ludhiana

After two years of our stay in Jalandhar we shifted to Ludhiana as the city was set up as a base for refugees from Sargodha. At that time I was studying in 10th. In Ludhiana, we lived in a huge house which was divided into two portions. One portion was occupied by us whereas another family resided in the other portion. The house's design was such that our toilet was located in the other family's portion. We had to cross their front door to use the toilet. It was odd but soon we got used to it.

In 1949 father was appointed as the minister for Health and Rehabilitation of Punjab. Shimla was the capital of Punjab. We shifted to Shimla where we lived in a bungalow called Charlie Villa, our official residence. Father worked very hard to rehabilitate the refugees. People who came from far off places to meet him, spent the night in a hall on the ground floor of the villa. Those who couldn't afford to eat outside were also served food. The entire day father was busy meeting people. His staff advised him not to work all the time and to take care of his health because he was a heart patient and his son was still a small boy. He would reply that he was only five when his own father died so if he could survive and reach to this position by the grace of God, wouldn't God help his son too?'

At that time I had just passed matric examination. Father wanted me to study in Kanya Mahavidyalaya Jalandhar which was a reputed college in north India. Besides academics, the college was known for its emphasis on patriotic values.

Hans Raj Mahila Mahavidyala was another good college in Jalandhar. Mahatma Hans Raj, a philanthropist had established a school for girls many years ago. In order to encourage girls to take admission in school, he introduced a scheme to gift a dupatta every six months and a one rupee coin every month to every girl student. In April 1950 , I took admission in Kanya Mahavidyalaya for class 11th (called FA- Faculty of Arts) in Jalandhar. Kumari Lajjawati was the principal of the college to whom we addressed as Achraya ji. As my parents lived in Shimla, I was put up in a hostel.

Father's last day : Dec 1, 1950 Ludhiana

They say the date and time of death is predestined. The death comes when our time is up. On Dec 1, 1950, father who was a minister of Health, was invited as a Chief Guest to inaugurate the children ward of Dayanand Medical College and hospital in Ludhiana. After the inauguration, he went on the stage to address the audience. He was a heart patient and his bodyguard always carried his medicine. During his address, father got a massive heart attack and collapsed. The bodyguard was standing just behind him. Even before the bodyguard could put the tablet in his mouth, father had passed away. It was strange that he was present in a hospital addressing the audience comprising well-known physicians and cardiologists and still he couldn't be saved. He was fifty-one years old.

His last words (said in Punjabi) - *mein aakhari saans tak esi tarah hi tuwadi sewa...*(I will be serving you till my last breath)

People came in thousands to pay their last respects to the departed soul. On the day of his funeral, the flyers were circulated with the following message from Sardar Vallabhbhai Patel, the first Home Minister and Deputy PM of India. '*Dr Lehna Singh Sethi who Lived and died in the service of homeless millions and saved them from dishonour and death*'

In Sabzi mandi area in Delhi, there is a market by the name of Lehna Singh Sethi. There is also Lehna Singh SD school in model town Ambala.

Father had earlier written to me that he would come to meet me on 1st December at my college. That fateful day, after the inauguration, he had planned to travel to Jalandhar. I was looking forward to meet him. I was studying in my hostel room when the principal summoned me. I presumed father had arrived but alas it was the news of his death.

Father lived his life on the twin principles of Selflessness and Empathy. Being my father's daughter, I've tried my best to live my life on his principles but I was not always successful.

I was very close to my father; he was my role model. His

death shattered me. I pretended to be normal but I was broken inside. I stopped smiling. For more than an year, I might not have smiled at all.

After father's demise, mother decided to settle down in Jalandhar because father's sister (Kartar Devi) lived there and mother was close to her. WG 527 Sarajganj Jalandhar was our new address. The house was allotted to us in lieu of a small piece of land father possessed in Sargodha. He had planned to build a house on it at a later stage. The market price of the house we got in Jalandhar was Rs 9500 which was higher than the value of the plot in Sargodha. The government wanted to give the house to us without charging any extra money but mother insisted she would pay the difference in instalments. She didn't believe in taking freebees because of her late husband's status.

The house in Sarajganj had been newly built by a Muslim family who fled to Pakistan during the riots. A few years after we had settled in that house, one morning we had a surprise visitor – a bunch of Muslim boys from Pakistan who were in Jalandhar to watch a cricket match. They were the original owners of the house who were curious to see their house. They went home happy that their house was well maintained and was now lived in by a family like them.

At the time of his death, father had only Rs 30 in his account. Since he had died in harness, the government sanctioned Rs 20,000 for our livelihood and education. From this fund which was to be managed by Charitable Endowments Department Punjab, mother was to be given Rs 250/month. Father also owned a car – a shiny white ambassador which he had bought on instalments. The final instalment was paid just a day before his death. According to the policy, those ministers who used their own vehicle were entitled for fuel reimbursement. The car was not needed now, it was sold for Rs 3200. Bua Kartar Devi's son Ramesh advised mother to invest the money in the stocks of a company. From this investment, she got Rs 150 monthly dividend. So mother had a monthly income of Rs 400 (Rs 250 from the government and Rs 150 as the dividend) which was enough to run the house and also pay my college fee, instalments of the house and Ravi's school fee. We were offered free education by the government but mother didn't accept it as she thought it to be humiliating. I left the hostel and became a day scholar.

By the time I finished post-graduation, the instalments of the house were over. When I started working, I took care of the household expenses and also paid for Ravi's education as the government grant was over by then. I offered to pay back the money to the government (Rs 250 monthly given to mother for our education) but my request was turned down.

Mother was forty-seven when father passed away. As far as my memory goes, I haven't seen her crying. Even if she was sad, she didn't show it and let it come in the way of her duties towards us. She was resilient, and prudent at managing the house with limited resources, never making us feel that we would now have to curtail our desires and stop dreaming. Ravi and I were aware of our means and didn't make unjust demands on her. Not only she brought us up well but she also tried to live her life. We too didn't feel anything lacking in our lives except father's presence.

DR. LEHNA SINGH

WHO

LIVED AND DIED IN THE SERCIVE OF HOMELESS MILLIONS AND SAVED THEM FROM DISHONOUR AND DEATH.

"A STOUT HEARTED AND BRAVE SON OF THE PUNJAB AND A LOYAL AND DISCIPLINED SOLDIER OF THE CONGRESS"

- SARDAR PATEL

Father (R) with Sardar Vallabhbhai Patel and his sister Maniben Patel in 1950

Father (centre) with Jawaharlal Nehru (left) in 1950

CHAPTER X

My College days

Jalandhar was a hub of education. There were three postgraduate colleges in Jalandhar – DAV college, Khalsa college and Doaba college, all were co-educational. I joined DAV college for post-graduation in Political Science. Not too many girls pursued post-graduation. The day classes and seminars were held at our respective colleges, and in the evening (5:00 p.m to 8:00 p.m) collective classes were conducted for the students of all the three colleges at Sai Das High school for Boys. A boy named Mohan was a student of Political Science at Doaba college; he attended collective classes in the evening with me. Mohan also happened to be my neighbour. His sister Indira was my friend and his younger brother was Ravi's friend. Whenever I could not find a particular book or paper in my college library, I would ask Mohan to get it for me from his college library. Mohan always obliged.

Once I wrote a paper on International Relations which was highly appreciated by the students and my college faculty. Mohan came home and asked me to share the paper with him, he said he would return it after reading but I refused point blank. Mother overheard us. After he left, she asked me the reason for my arrogance.

'This is not arrogance, I don't like this exchange of notes,' I said, a cold expression on my face.

Mother was agitated. 'Where such thoughts go when you make your demands on him?' she said, and commanded me to give him the paper which of course I did.

Another similar incident reminds me of mother's trust in

me. It was the last day of college before the summer vacation. I was the last to come out from the classroom only to find a boy waiting for me. I had never spoken to him before. He politely asked if he could come to my house to exchange some books and notes. Those days students of opposite gender didn't mingle with each other outside the classrooms though inside the classroom they interacted. If a boy and girl were seen even talking to each other outside the class, people assumed they were having an affair, and the pair would be the butt of a joke.

'Most welcome,' I replied. He asked for my address which I gave promptly. Later when I narrated the incident to my friend Lata, she was furious. 'First he'll borrow the book then he'll come to return it with a love letter in it, then again you'll give him the book with a reply to his love letter, and this process will go on, and you will be the subject of gossip for the neighbours.'

I was petrified. My father's reputation was precious to me. I would never do anything which would bring a blot to my father's name. In my nervousness I was unable to even ride the cycle back home. Somehow I reached home out of breath. I told mother I had made a blunder by giving my address to a boy, and narrated the incident to her. Her reaction surprised me pleasantly. 'If someone comes with good intentions, let him come, but if his intention is bad, I'll see to it. You needn't worry,' she said patting my back. 'You just focus on your studies.' I don't know if it was the telepathy or my prayers, that boy never came home.

An unpleasant episode from my college days still pricks my conscious. Once during my exam days, mother fell sick, so the responsibility of the entire household fell on me. At the same time mother's cousin Kishen Singh visited us on his way back from Amritsar. He had brought a piece of cloth with him to stitch an underwear as he had lost his undergarment during his travels. He asked mother for the sewing machine to stitch his undergarment. Instead of showing him where the machine was, mother said, 'Sharda'll stitch it for you'. I was washing clothes outside. Upon hearing her, I lost my cool. I bombarded into the room, a big frown on my face. 'I'm working the whole day, hardly getting time to study for my exams, over and above you make me stitch people's clothes. If I fail, you will blame me for not studying well,' I yelled.

First mother was speechless, then she started crying. I stood there for a while and watched her cry profusely. On retrospection I had a guilt feeling about my outburst. I don't remember if I did the stitching or not, but I took a vow never to raise my voice again, and to hurt her. Her anguished face flashes before my eyes whenever I recollect that incident. That was the only time in my life I saw her cry bitterly.

Once during my college days, Congress Seva Dal organized a three-week residential camp for girls at Chandrawatiganj in Madhya Pradesh. The parents of a former Prime Minister Satish Gujral - Avtar Narayan Gujral and Pushpa Gujral, both freedom fighters, were our family friends. Pushpa Gujral recommended me for this camp. I was one of the two students from Jalandhar who were selected to participate in the camp. We were a group of twenty girls who had come from various parts of the country.

We were taught life skills such as discipline, bravery etc. At night the girls slept on the floor in the covered veranda. Every night, two girls stood guards. Once it was my duty. We were taking rounds of the place, when we spotted a snake in the veranda. Before we could alert the sleeping girls, we watched in horror the snake sneak into a girl's shirt from one side and come out from the other. It was a horrifying sight.

Jawahar Lal Nehru: My fan girl moment

A few months later, Congress party had its annual session in Jalandhar. PM Jawahar Lal Nehru was to address the gathering. The girls trained by Congress Seva Dal were chosen to be the volunteers for the function. My duty was near the stage exit. Nehru ji was to climb on the stage from one end, deliver his speech and come down from the other end. As per the plan, Nehru ji climbed the stage and mesmerized the audience with his inspiring speech. I eagerly waited for him to come down from the stage. The moment his speech ended, I straightened myself to greet him. Suddenly a party worker called him; he about turned and started walking away from me. On realizing that I had lost my fan girl moment to meet him, I left my position on the stage and ran after him. Stopping just behind him, I touched his shoulder lightly. He turned around. 'Yes beta?' he asked.

In my nervousness I forgot the script. 'Please bless me so that I walk on your footsteps,' I managed to say.

'Yes, it would be like this only,' he said, walking away.

For the rest of the day I stayed in a dazed state. My life long wish to see him in person and greet him had been fulfilled. I didn't wash my hand for the rest of the day.

CHAPTER XI

My work : My passion

Most girls got married after matriculation or graduation. Those who pursued post-graduation did so either because they hadn't yet found a good match or wanted to seek employment. Mother was a progressive woman. Education of her children was her priority. In those times, marriage of the daughter was the biggest worry for parents but mother was different. She had no marriage plans for me. She was not even ready to consider any marriage proposal until my MA exams were over. In fact she wanted me to pursue LLB so that I could fight for the rights of women and cases of domestic abuse and dowry but law didn't interest me, I'd always wanted to be a working woman, and was interested in a field job where I could serve the society.

After finishing MA in 1957, I got the job of a lecturer in a newly opened SD college on Tanda Road, Jalandhar city. I accepted the job offer but my heart was in the field work.

Those days, teaching and medical professions were the preferred fields for girls. I wanted to become a doctor and serve the rural folks but that was not to be as I wasn't good at Math and Science so I had to pursue Humanities group. My keenness to experience the village life attracted me towards field job. The real India lives in villages, the government slogan said but such jobs were not considered appropriate for women because it involved a lot of touring, and staying away from home for days together.

The Department of Public relations had just started appointing women for the field jobs. Even before I got the job of a lecturer, I had written to Sardar Partap Singh

Kairon, the then Chief Minister of Punjab and a close friend of father about the field service. Once, Sardar Partap Singh Kairon was admitted in a hospital at Amritsar for some nose ailment. Ravi and I went to the hospital to see him. He asked me if I have got any information about my job from Bibi Prakash Kaur, the Health Minister of Punjab as he had entrusted her the task of finding a job for me. I told him that she was arranging a job for me in Development department but I have come to know that village folks are not good people. He laughed and said, 'Don't people know you are Kairon's daughter? If anyone casts an evil eye on you, I will gouge his eyes out.' He was a gentleman who considered daughter of his ex-colleague as his own.

I worked as a college lecturer for only one and a half months and hadn't yet got my first salary (Rs 150/month) when the offer came for a job in Public Relations department. I grabbed it. A monthly salary of Rs 250 (which was huge) was not even an attraction, I was fascinated with serving the rural folks. I had to lose my salary due from the college because I had left the job without prior notice.

My first job

June 12, 1958. I joined my first job as District Publicity Supervisor in Public Relations department Jalandhar. DPRO (District Public Relations Officer) Shri Pargat Singh was my first boss, my first mentor and guide in professional life. Besides me there were three Publicity Supervisors, all male. At that time I was the only woman employee in the office but I didn't feel odd. There were no separate toilets for women, only a common toilet with a door and bolt for the entire staff. There were also no separate cabins for the field staff, they would come to the office, mark their attendance in the register and leave. They were not required to sit in the office the whole day. Whether they went out for publicity work or for personal work, no one knew. My boss didn't feel appropriate for me to roam around like others, he felt protective towards me and considered himself my guardian perhaps because of my lineage. He asked me not to go to any clerical staff for any work or for taking my salary (salary was given in cash), I should gracefully sit in my cabin. If needed, I should call the staff to my desk.

Now he felt the need to have a separate cabin for the field staff. Until the cabin was ready, he asked me to sit in front of him and write down every word spoken by him to any staff member or visitor which was a huge learning experience for me. He also educated me about public dealings. After four days, the cabin for publicity supervisors was ready.

It felt great to be a working woman. When I was in school, there lived a family in neighbourhood whose two daughters were working women. Before going to office, they would call out to their mother, 'Mata ji, we're going to office.' I longed for a day when I too would say the same words to my mother. And when that day arrived, I felt I was living my dream.

I had always been very excited about touring but when the time came, I realized it wasn't as easy as I had expected it to be. I was afraid of travelling alone. It was rare for women to travel alone. Mother encouraged me by assuring that if needed she would travel with me but of course it was not practical to do that every time, so I hired a woman from local Gandhi Vanita ashram to travel along with me on tours as a companion. Her services were needed only during my tours. I would pay her Re 1 per day and also take care of her bus fare and food. It was actually quite an expensive affair. My department gave my TA (Travel Allowance) but not my companion's.

After a month Miss Sarla Prashar, a smart middle-aged woman was transferred to Jalandhar, and I was delighted to have some female company. She later became a minister but unfortunately once while on an official tour, she met with an accident and died.

My boss told me Miss Sarla Prashar's ultimate motive was to join politics, this job in Public Relations was a step for her to get connected with people at the ground level. He asked me not to go with her anywhere without his prior permission.

One day Miss Sarla Prashar who was a divorcee made a program to show cinema to the jail inmates. One of the responsibilities of the public relations department was to educate and enlighten public through cinema, lectures and plays. The program was in the evening. She instructed me to join her and left. I rushed to my boss to seek his permission. He refused outright. I was in a dilemma. I didn't know what excuse to make for not joining her. I thought of an excuse (which looked genuine), that my brother who was to accompany me to the jail had returned home late after playing, so I couldn't come.

Next day when we met in the office, I had just started to say the already rehearsed excuse when she interrupted me. 'Sharda! Good that you didn't come, the jail Superintendent didn't allow me to accompany the cinema party inside the jail because there were hardcore criminals and they couldn't take risk with the ladies.' Breathing a sigh of relief, I decided to save that excuse for future.

At that time in Punjab the Betterment tax was levied on

the farmers. Obviously they were agitated. Noormahal in Jalandhar district was a much disturbed area due to farmers' agitations. The government was doing its best to calm down the farmers and bring home the logic to them that the Betterment tax was for their benefit but the agitations continued.

Along with other related departments like Agriculture and Development, the field staff of Public Relations department was deputed to hold public meetings in the areas hit by agitations and address gatherings to explain government policies to people. I was asked to travel to Noormahal. By then Miss Sarla Prashar was already transferred from Jalandhar so only my arrangement of stay at Noormahal had to be made. There were no hotels or guest houses in that area and even if there were, it was unheard of a woman staying alone in a hotel. The DPRO organized my stay at the house of a well-known Joshi family which comprised grandmother, sons, daughters-in-law and their children.

Being a woman has its own perks. I didn't have to go anywhere, my staff of three-four men colleagues would hold meetings with the people and come to me in the evening to give the report which I would submit to the DPRO. I stayed with that family for a week, accomplished my duty gracefully. They took care of me very well. It must have caused them discomfort but they accommodated me graciously.

As a part of my job, I conducted meetings to educate village women folks about girl child education, adult education, small savings, family planning and such other subjects. After every tour, I had to prepare the report and present to the boss. We had to send monthly reports to the head office through DPRO. Once the head office clerk found out that in my reports, the subject of family planning was never mentioned. A show cause notice was sent to me about this. I replied that because I myself was unmarried and didn't know anything about family planning so how could I educate others on this topic. The subjects like sex education were a taboo in schools and colleges. My honest confession was much appreciated by my boss and no further questions were asked.

My experience with villagers was phenomenal. The villagers gave me a lot of respect. There were no roadside dhabas or restaurants. The village folks were so hospitable that I didn't have to carry my own food. They served me and my team delicious food and took care of us very well.

Once at a guest house I was waiting to receive a minister when I met a middle-aged woman named Hardeep Kaur who had come to meet the minister regarding a job. We started chatting. It so happened that the minister didn't turn up but Hardeep Kaur had a job. I gave her a job in my department as my assistant for a salary of Rs 25/month. She was enthusiastic about her work, was energetic and had good public relations skills. She proved to be of immense help to me during my village tours.

The woman I had hired earlier was just a companion but Hardeep Kaur was my assistant in the true sense. Whenever we visited a village, she did not allow me to roam around. I would stay put at the house of sarpanch whereas Hardeep Kaur would go around from house to house to inform the women about the meetings. She would tell them a young girl has come to meet them. If a woman was giving bath to a child, Hardeep Kaur would take over and ask the woman to get ready so in a short time I would have a large number of women as my audience.

Hardeep Kaur knew how to motivate people to attend meetings and functions. She worked with me till my transfer to Ambala. Later she became a friend to my mother and also to my mother-in-law.

I worked for one and a half years before I got married. I continued to work after marriage. There was no question or discussion on if I would be allowed to work after marriage. Life just continued as earlier except the change of my address and last name.

CHAPTER XII

A match made in heaven

I didn't want to get married to a lecturer but it was written in the stars that I would get married to a lecturer and so I did. A close friend of father, Sardar Amar Singh (I addressed him as Chacha ji), took it upon himself to find a suitable boy for me. Chacha ji who hailed from Sargodha, was posted in Jalandhar as a Sessions judge at that time. His wife Mehtab Kaur (Chachi ji) often discussed my marriage plans with mother. They had two daughters and three sons. Their eldest daughter Bhupinder Kaur (Bhupi) is six years younger to me. Chacha ji was keen on finding a lecturer boy for me because he said lecturers are usually devoid of any bad habits and such a boy would be most suitable for our simple family.

When I got the whiff of the discussions going on in the house, I told mother upfront that I didn't want to marry a lecturer but she said your Chacha ji is trying to find only a lecturer match. I kept mum.

A few days later, one day Ravi and I visited Chacha ji's house in Model Town. When we were entering their house, Bhupi's tutor was coming out of the house. He was bald. I got an opportunity to vent out my feelings against lecturers. 'What's the life of these poor professors, they become bald at a young age,' I said to Chacha ji.

He laughed and rebuked me for talking such things about lecturers.

Destiny brought us together

Bhupi's mama ji, Sardar Anup Singh was a close friend of Yash ji's mausa ji Ramsaran Batra. Anup Singh happened to meet Yash ji at a family function at Ramsaran Batra's house in Delhi. Yash ji had gone there with his mother. Bhupi's mama ji inquired about the boy from Batra ji who said the boy in question was the son of his sister-in-law, and was working as a lecturer in Mandi Dabwali (now in Haryana). 'Will this boy suit Dr Sahib's daughter?' Anup Singh asked Batra ji.

Batra ji was elated at the proposal but he didn't want to commit on behalf of his sister-in-law's family. At home he discussed the matter with Beeji and Bauji (Yash ji's parents and later more than my parents) and it was an instant yes from them.

Yash ji's family was invited to Amar Singh chacha ji's house in Jalandhar for the girl viewing ceremony. No one had said a word to me about this. It was a Sunday and I was getting ready to go for a movie named Adalat with my friends. I was ironing my clothes when chacha ji's peon came to call me. Mother asked me if I could cancel the movie program and instead go to their house, I readily agreed. At that time Ravi was doing post-graduation in Dehradun and was not at home. I took out my cycle and left for Model town. When I reached their house, I saw Bhupi carrying a jug of lassi from the kitchen to the dining room. 'Who has come to your house?' I asked her.

'Children of Papa ji's friend have come for lunch,' she replied thrusting the jug in my hand. I carried the jug inside. At the dining table, a young man and three young girls were having lunch with chacha ji and chachi ji. The three young girls were Yash ji's sisters - Chander, Sudesh

(Chander's best friend) and Suresh. I had no inclination that this was the boy's party who had come to see me. I pulled a chair; we chatted casually and the discussion steered towards women's rights. Chacha ji posed a question to me,

'These days girls want equality, what's your opinion?'

'We don't want equality, we want cooperation, coordination and friendship,' I replied confidently.

I saw the eyeballs rolling.

Chacha ji asked me how as a PR professional I would advise people to resolve the issue of shortage of food in our country?

I had no idea these questions were being asked to showcase me to the boy and his family. 'People should reduce their food consumption so that it could reach more people,' I replied earnestly.

At this, Yash ji looked in my direction and the morsel of food that was on the way to his mouth stopped mid-air.

A week later, Amar Singh chacha ji received a letter from Yash ji's father. The question of asking the girl's opinion in the matters of her marriage didn't occur in our times. If elders thought it was the right choice for me, indeed it was right. Anyway the boy looked to be decent and was handsome so I had no objection to the alliance. I am sure if I had an objection, mother wouldn't have gone ahead with the proposal.

A few days later, Ravi was sent to Siwani (a small town near Hisar in Haryana where Yash ji's parents lived) to meet the boy and his family. He didn't want to go as he said, if everyone was okay with the boy, what was there for him to see. Chacha ji intervened, 'if you see the boy anywhere, you wouldn't even recognize him, so go see the boy and also meet the family.' Ravi planned a trip to Siwani for two days but returned after four days overwhelmed by the hospitality, love and warmth showered on him by my future family.

The Suitable boy

On November 21, 1959 I got married to Yash Gulati, son of Dr Chaman Lal Gulati, a medico by profession and Suhagwanti (maiden name Bharawan). My father-in-law was posted at the government dispensary in Siwani. The family consisted of parents, four sons, three daughters, and paternal grandmother named Billo. The eldest brother Bhimsen had gone to Canada to study FRCS after doing MBBS, and was still unmarried. Yash ji, the second eldest sibling had done MA in Hindi from Government college for Boys Ludhiana and was posted in Khalsa college at Mandi Dabwali as a lecturer. The next in line were three beautiful sisters - Chander, Raj and Suresh. Chander and Suresh were studying at Government college for girls Ludhiana and were in hostel. The two younger brothers - Surinder and Anil , always full of mischief were studying in school in Siwani. Raj, the middle sister, after doing matric and Teachers' training was at home in Siwani.

Yash ji was the first in the line of siblings to get married. For the marriage, my in-laws had rented a house in Ludhiana for a month as it was close to Jalandhar. Moreover Ludhiana was a familiar city for them because in early days Beeji used to live there for the education of the older children. There were no schools in Siwani other than primary. Ludhiana was known for good education.

After our marriage in Jalandhar, the family went back to Siwani with the new bride. Every night after dinner, we sat together in one of the three rooms and chatted about anything and everything. I equally participated in the discussions. No one expected the new bride to be coy. Bauji's dispensary was located just outside the house so he too would come home early. My in-laws were aware of the sacrifices my father had made for the country. They had great regard for him and everyone wanted to know more about him.

One evening, I was narrating the incidents from Pita ji's life. While talking about his death, I couldn't control myself and burst into tears. I started crying. Beeji was reminded of her loss as she had lost her father at a very tender age and could relate to my pain more than anyone else. She too began to cry. To console me, she took me in her bosom and both of us cried. That night, I felt a strange bond with my mother-in-law. We became very close and with time the bond only strengthened.

No dowry was asked/given in my marriage

I believe giving dowry to a girl in her marriage diminishes her dignity. It was my strong wish to get married to a boy who had the same values as mine about dowry. My unspoken wish was heard by the almighty. At the time of my engagement, thals of sweets and baskets of fruits, were kept ready to be given as shagun but my would be in-laws refused to accept anything. Later the sweets and fruits were distributed to the neighbours.

At the time of marriage, mother got a few silk sarees and suits for me, and also the clothes for the boy and his family. Everything was turned down by the groom's family. The following day I visited mother's house for pag phera. (a ritual where the bride visits her parents' home for the first time after marriage), While returning to my marital home

I carried a suitcase full of clothes which had already been purchased for me. On return my father-in-law saw an extra suitcase and called me in a corner and said, 'I'd thought you're my daughter but you've remained of Sethis' only.'

Next time I went to mother's house and returned the suitcase. In my marriage, I had taken only a gold necklace set and two kadas which mother insisted that I must take. In the war of 1962, I donated a gold ring and one of the kadas to the war fund.

After marriage, Yash ji returned to Mandi Dabwali where he worked, and I stayed back in Jalandhar and continued living with mother. He didn't want to settle down in Mandi Dabwali because it was notorious as a wet area. He was looking for a new job in some other city. After six months he found a job at Khalsa college for girls in Jalandhar. After one year, my father-in-law got himself transferred to Civil hospital in Jalandhar city. Chander and Suresh also left Ludhiana and got admission in Jalandhar so we all lived together as a big happy family. Only the eldest brother Bhimsen was overseas and hadn't yet got married. My grand mother-in-law had passed away by then.

I had always wished for a husband with a romantic name

Three years before my marriage, my cousin Krishna got married to a boy named Surinder. Once when I visited her in Delhi, I noticed that she addressed her husband by his name. Just the thought of calling the husband by name fascinated me. I thought it to be very romantic. I wished my future husband had a nice name so that I could also call him by name but when the time came, I never called Yash ji by name. Those days it was rare for women to address their husbands by name.

It so happened that a few days after marriage, one evening in Siwani I was sitting with the women of the family. I saw this an opportunity to get over the hesitation of calling my husband by name. I started narrating a random incident just to take his name but instead of his name, I said 'Professor Sahib was telling....' In my mind, I laughed, he was a professor for his students and not for me. I tried again, I started talking something and this time I was sure I would take his name and I said 'Yash ji was saying....'

Everyone was dumbfounded. I couldn't tell if they had approved of my act. My grand mother-in-law (addressed as Bhabhi ji) was also around. Putting a finger on her lips, a surprised expression on her face, she said, '*Kudi, na payi leni?* (Girl, you're taking your husband's name?)'

I let out an embarrassed laugh.

'Happily take his name, times are changing,' Bhabhi ji said lovingly. But I was so conscious for the whole of my life that I couldn't take his name and fulfil my wish. Even Yash ji never called me by my name. While addressing each other, we would just start the conversation without prefixes, any endearing words or each other's name.

• • •

The newlyweds with Mata ji and Ravi at Jalandhar on Nov 21, 1959

With my Suitable boy

In 1959, at Ludhiana - two days after our wedding
Standing L-R: Anil, Chander, Raj, Sudesh, Suresh and Surinder
Sitting L-R: Bauji, Beeji, Bhabhi ji (paternal grandmother), Yours truly and Yash ji

CHAPTER XIII

Our first born

Neetu, our eldest daughter was born in Jalandhar one and a half year after our marriage. Being the first child in the next generation, she was pampered by her dada, dadi, Buas and Chachas. After the maternity leave ended and I joined back work, Beeji managed the house and also the baby. Even if there was a helper, the complete responsibility of the baby fell on my mother-in-law.

She would give her bath, and then massage her. I had seen that the kids were massaged before bath and they looked very happy so I always wondered why the other way round. Once I asked Beeji why not massage before the bath as was the practice. She replied that it didn't suit our children. I laughed in my mind. Children were children, what was so different about the children of our family.

On one Saturday, Beeji had to go to a kirtan and the charge of giving bath to Neetu was on me as it was a holiday. I got a chance to try my belief. I gave her a nice massage, she giggled and then I gave her bath. For the entire day, she was playful but at night she coughed a little which was nothing to be worried of. The following morning, Beeji had to go somewhere again and I did the same and enjoyed my baby's giggles.

That night, Neetu fell sick, so sick that she couldn't breathe properly. She had got pneumonia. At midnight, Bauji who was a medical practitioner, wrote the prescription and Yash ji was sent to the chemist shop to fetch the medicines. It was night and he was not yet familiar with the city. He hired a rickshaw and somehow located a pharmacy.

At home Neetu's condition worsened. Bauji gave her five injections one after another.By morning she started showing signs of improvement. I heaved a sigh of relief but I had a feeling of guilt as it had happened because of my experimentation of massage before bath. Later I confessed to Beeji about it.

Transfer to Ambala

Yash ji was MA in Hindi but he always wanted to study further. From the very beginning of his career his goal was to be a faculty in university so he enrolled himself for MA in English and also got registered for PhD in Hindi. In mid 1961, he applied to SD College Ambala for teaching post-graduate classes but was not selected. A few months later, another vacancy arose in the same college and he was selected. He packed his bags and left for Ambala.

Mr Avinash Chandra Bali was the news editor of The Tribune which was published from Ambala at that time. Later in 1980, The Tribune was shifted to Chandigarh. It's still the most popular newspaper in Chandigarh and surrounding areas. Mr Bali had a great respect for my father and he was also instrumental in Yash ji's appointment to SD college. Our other well-wisher was Mr Roshan Lal Verma, a freedom fighter, who was Director Public Relations Punjab and my ultimate boss. At that time mostly those who were associated with the freedom movement in any way were appointed in the public relations department.

Mr Bali and Mr Verma were thick friends. Mr Bali on his own took the task of my transfer to Ambala without even informing me. It was understood that if husband works in Ambala, wife would join him.He told Mr Verma that our son-in-law has joined SD college Ambala and now our daughter should be transferred there. I would've tried for the transfer at a later stage but I didn't want it immediately because Neetu was only six months old and I had a great support system in my in-laws.

January 23, 1962. I was on tour that day. In the evening when I came back, Beeji informed me that someone had come from my office with the instruction that I should talk to my boss DPRO G.S Randhir immediately.

Like most people, we didn't have a telephone at home. The only telephone in the street was at the house of Raj Chopra, one of Ravi's very good friends. I knocked at Raj Chopra's house and called my boss. Even before I could say hello, my boss spoke, 'We considered you as our daughter but you deceived us. I didn't expect this from you...'

I wondered what wrong I had done to earn his wrath. I said I had gone to the village and had taken due permission for the tour but he said he was not talking about the tour. 'Without informing me, you have got yourself transferred to Ambala.'

I was shocked. 'I haven't made such a request,' I replied. 'My daughter is very small. I can't afford to go anywhere without my in-laws.'

If that was the case then he suggested that I should get the transfer orders cancelled. He told me Mr Hans Raj Sharma, the minister-in-charge of our department was to visit Phagwara the following day and recommended that I should meet him personally and request for the cancellation of my transfer order. When I informed my in-laws about it, they asked me to accept the transfer. 'It will be an insult to the noble soul who had made efforts for your transfer even without your request,' Bauji said. He was right, ultimately I had to join my husband so why not now. My in-laws offered to keep Neetu with them in case it was difficult for me to take care of the baby but I decided to take her with me.

CHAPTER XIV

A Happening life in Ambala (Jan 1962 - Nov 18, 1971)

Ambala was the second station of my posting where we lived for ten years before moving to Rohtak. For about seven years I worked in the position of District Publicity Supervisor which is second in command to DPRO. Sardar Trilochan Singh was the DPRO and my immediate boss. He was a wonderful person and gave due respect to his subordinates. In his absence, if his signatures were required on any urgent paper, he would ask me to sign on his behalf. Four years later, on Nov 1, 1966, Haryana was carved out of Punjab and made a separate state. I was allocated to Haryana state because I was already serving in Ambala which was a part of Haryana. Yash ji worked at SD college in Ambala so it suited us fine. Sardar Tricholan Singh was transferred to Patiala and in his place came Mr Kanti Chandra Sain who was just the opposite of my previous boss, and with whom working was never smooth. He was vindictive in nature and most employees had problems with him. Adjacent to my boss' room was my room which I shared with my peers - Comrade Gurmukh Singh, S.D Sharda and Kirori Shah.

Once I was on a casual leave for three days, in my absence our room was changed. I was surprised none of the supervisors had objected to the change. The new room allotted to us was just opposite to the room of the drama party. The drama party had ten performers who rehearsed loudly and made a lot of noise the entire day. It was difficult to concentrate on work. When I returned from leave and learnt about the change of rooms, I walked into DPRO's office and explained to him our problem in as polite words as possible.

'Whatever it is, done is done,' he said calmly.

'Then I've nothing more to say,' I replied and came back to my room.

He took it as my bluntness. After a few days I proceeded on maternity leave and at the same time he received his transfer orders. Before leaving, he decided to teach me a lesson for my bluntness and recommended my transfer to Narnaul, an interior area of Haryana. He knew that my husband also worked in Ambala. When maternity leave got over and I re-joined, I pulled some strings and got my transfer orders cancelled and continued working at Ambala.

Mr Eshwar Chandra Gupta was the new DPRO. His stay was short, and after his transfer, I was given the charge of acting DPRO that meant performing all the duties of DPRO without any financial powers. Before making any expenditure, I had to take prior approval from the head office in Chandigarh. I wanted the DPRO's phone to be installed at my residence so that I could carry out my additional responsibilities with ease but I was told according to the policy, an acting officer is not entitled to the phone at the residence. Left with no choice, I carried out my functions.

Mr B.S. Ojha was the Deputy Commissioner Ambala. When I took the charge of acting DPRO, I was told by the staff that the previous DPROs used to go to the DC's house every morning to apprise him of the news published in the daily newspapers concerning the district. It felt odd. I didn't know if I was expected to follow the footsteps of my predecessors, I decided to check with the boss. I picked up the phone and after greeting him, asked if like Gupta ji, I too am expected to come to his residence every morning to brief him about the news. The DC was embarrassed. 'No Mrs Gulati, you don't need to do that. I'll call you myself if you are needed here.'

The other tradition of not having phone at home was also broken during the tenure of Mr Ojha. Those days the office timings changed with seasons. In summers the timings were from 7:00 a.m. to 1:30 p.m., and 9.00 a.m. to 5.00 p.m. in winters. Once in summers, Mr Ojha had to discuss an urgent matter with me. The office had already closed by then. He rang the office and asked the watchman to inform me to call him immediately. The office was in the city and my residence was in Model Town. The watchman came home on his bicycle. I went to some neighbour's house to make the call. In the process, more than an hour was wasted. I apologized for the delay and explained to the DC the reason for the delay. 'Where is the phone which was at Gupta's residence?' he asked.

'Sir, I can't have that phone at my residence because I'm an acting DPRO,' I replied.

'What nonsense?' he said.

After two hours, the lineman was installing the phone at my residence. This was the first case in the state of Haryana when many DPROs didn't have a phone at their residence but an officiating DPRO had.

A few months later, I was promoted to the position of DPRO (District Public Relation Officer). I was responsible for the publicity of the government in the entire district. Mr Ojha was transferred and in his place Mr S.K Sharma, a young unmarried man joined as deputy commissioner. Even before meeting him personally an episode happened. One morning, I received a call from my head office at

Chandigarh that in the evening Mr R.S Verma, director Public Relations was arriving at Ambala with the press party. I was asked to inform the new DC to meet the director and also the media at the Ambala rest house. I rang up and conveyed the message to the new DC personally. After about two hours there was another call from the head office that the evening program had been cancelled and the same had to be conveyed to the DC. I rang up DC's office. The phone was answered by his PA who took the message and promised to convey to his boss about it. That evening it rained heavily. At home, my phone rang and on the other side was Mr Sharma, the new Deputy Commissioner. 'What the hell? Where is Mr Verma and his press party.' I was stunned. 'Sir, his visit is cancelled. Haven't you received the message?'

'To whom did you give the message? I never got any message.'

I understood that his PA must have forgotten to give the message but I didn't want to take the PA's name. 'Sir, I gave the message but you consider this as my fault.'

The DC didn't insist either. 'In future, feel free to talk to me personally,' he said before disconnecting the call.

The next day PA apologized for the goof up. He was near retirement and the nature of the new boss wasn't yet known so I didn't want to spoil the rest of his tenure but I learnt a lesson that important matters are to be communicated to the boss directly without fear and hesitation.

By-elections in 1971

The public relations department is assigned the task of publicity for the ruling party even though it is illegal to use the government machinery and equipment for the promotion of the party. At the time of by-elections in Narayangarh subdivision, our department started the publicity of the party but it had to be done discreetly. As a part of procedure and also to claim the TA, we had to enter the details of the places we toured in the logbook. We were instructed not to write the actual name of the place we visited and instead just fill in any random name in the logbook. The bureaucrats and the officers didn't like promoting the political candidates for the elections but there was hardly a choice for them. Once the CM had to address a public rally at Narayangarh subdivision. I was supervising the rally arrangements when one of the party workers casually asked me which all places we have covered so far.

'This is our personal matter,' I replied promptly.

Later I realized this may go against me so I decided to apprise the DC about it. DC, SP and other officers had already arrived for the CM's rally and were waiting at the residence of Miss Veena Kohli, the Sub divisional officer of Narayangarh. Her residence was at some distance from the venue of the rally. There were special orders that department's jeeps and vehicles were not to be seen near the venue so I ran through the fields to the SDM's residence. I was breathless when I reached. The officers were sitting on the charpais in the front yard. 'What happened Mrs Gulati, why're you running?' the DC Mr S.K. Sharma sounded nervous. I told Mr Sharma about the incident and he jumped from the cot. 'Please tell repeatedly to those idiots that it's our personal matter,' he said, laughing.

In some time the rally began. The party worker who was anchoring the show was not well prepared, he was forgetting his lines, and was fumbling. It was annoying. My hands ached to grab the mike from him and anchor the show but the DC asked me to sit back and watch these buffoons conduct the show. In some time the rally ended, and we packed off.

There is another co-worker who comes to my mind as I write about my tenure in Ambala. Satya Narayan, the stage master of our drama party, was a burly young man always ready to pick up a fight. He belonged to Rohtak and had been transferred to Ambala on a complaint. He hadn't taken any room or house on rent for himself so at night he slept in one of the rooms in the office. Strangely he would always sleep with a gun under his arm. The entire office was scared of him because of his gun.

Since the dialect changes every few kilometres, the actors of the drama party were posted closer to their native place so that the public follows them easily. For the artist too, his act is more effective if it is delivered in his own dialect. Ambala was a Punjabi speaking area, and Satya Narayan's dialect was Haryanvi so he hadn't been accepted well as people had difficulty understanding his dialect. He was a good actor but because of his Haryanvi dialect he failed to make a mark and had become a laughing stock amongst people. He loved performing on the stage but his fellow actors wouldn't allow him because public would start hooting the moment he climbed the stage so there was always a tussle between him and other actors.

I decided to speak to my boss about getting him transferred back to Rohtak but before I could do so, Mrs Sharda Rani, the Chief Parliamentary Secretary in-charge of our department and my namesake visited our office for inspection. I decided to talk to her about Satya Narayan's transfer. I weaved a story and told Mrs Sharda Rani that

Satya Narayan was a good performer but his talent was being wasted in Ambala because public made fun of him as they didn't understand his language so he should be transferred back to Rohtak. The same evening his transfer orders were issued which brought a relief to Satya Narayan as well as to the Ambala staff.

Nanny for my daughters

1965. My in-laws had been staying with us since Neetu's birth. They took care of her with a lot of love. They continued to live with us even after Bittu was born. Bittu was only a few months old when Bauji got himself transferred to Siwani, he wanted to live there before his retirement. Beeji too had to join him but she wanted to leave only after satisfactory arrangement had been made for the children so I started looking for a nanny. Neetu who was already in school, got worried when I told her that Beeji would be leaving soon. 'Who would look after Bittu and me,' she would ask repeatedly. I wanted to hire a middle-aged woman as nanny so I told her, we have a Maa ji who has gone somewhere, she would come back soon and take care of you.

I sent a request to Employment Exchange to find a nanny for me. Raj Rani, a middle-aged woman had enrolled herself in the Employment Exchange. One day Raj Rani went to inquire about her job application, she was told there was a house job available if she was interested. She didn't care which job, she just wanted any job. Straight from the Employment Exchange office, she came to our residence. Crisp cotton saree over plump frame, round face, a red bindi dotting her broad forehead, lips red from paan chewing, oily hair tied in a neat bun at the back of her head,

I was delighted to see a well-dressed woman for the job of a nanny. Raj Rani demanded a monthly salary of Rs 35. I tried to negotiate saying I would be spending on her meals also but she was clear, she wouldn't accept a paisa less than thirty five. She didn't mind bringing her own food.

Just at that time Neetu returned from school and looked at the stranger sitting on the cot with me. 'Neetu, she is your Maa ji,' I said to my daughter.

Neetu jumped into her lap and cried with joy. 'Maa ji, where were you for so many days?'

I thought if the nanny brought her own food, Neetu would wonder what kind of Maa ji was this who was bringing her own food. So the deal was struck for a monthly salary of Rs 35 and two meals a day. We lived near Jagadhri Gate, and her house was at a walking distance.

Raj Rani would come in the morning carrying a cane basket containing her paan box; her cotton saree starched and neatly pinned. She would change into another saree for house wear and take charge of the house and kids. In the evening when I reached home, she would be wheeling the pram on the road. Before leaving she would again change into her starched saree. Raj Rani was efficient in her work and good with children. With her around, I didn't have to worry about housework and kids.

When we shifted to Model town, she asked for a hike and demanded a salary of Rs 65 as she had to commute by bus and also take care of another child (In 1967, our youngest daughter Guria was born) but I was not willing to give her such a high raise. I tried finding another nanny but when I couldn't find anyone who would fit in my requirement and was as loving and efficient as Raj Rani, I agreed to give her what she wanted. Moreover, I thought if I could afford a good nanny for the older two daughters, it would be a huge injustice to the third one if I didn't have a good nanny for her too. Raj Rani worked with us till we shifted to Rohtak.

A horrifying incident from Neetu's childhood

When Neetu was four years old, she went to Siwani to be with her grandparents. After a few days I went to Siwani with six-month-old Bittu to bring Neetu back. I stayed there for a week. While coming back, like always I had more luggage than I had brought. Apart from my own stuff (a trunk of clothes, boxes of sweets and a bedroll), I had bought two large tins of pure ghee for my neighbours. The women in my neighbourhood wanted me to get pure ghee for them as the ghee in Siwani was cheaper and of high quality.

There was no direct train from Siwani to Ambala. The train had to be changed at Hisar. I was used to travelling, so changing trains with two children and the luggage was not a problem for me. Bauji sent his peon with me to see me off till Hisar with strict instructions to him that he should return only after settling me in the direct train to Ambala.

It was midnight when the train from Siwani reached Hisar junction. It was dark and the platform was deserted. There was still some time left for my train to arrive. I waited on a bench with children, my luggage kept nearby.

Meanwhile the train to Siwani arrived and the peon asked me if he could leave as his next train was only in the morning. I was furious. Why had he come with me if he wanted to leave me alone? I could've commanded him to follow the instructions of his boss but in anger I asked him to leave. The moment his train left, there was an announcement on the public address system that the train to Ambala wouldn't come to the platform and the passengers would have to board the train from the railway yard where the train was parked. The railway yard was at some distance. I called a porter. The luggage couldn't be carried by a single porter in one round. I don't remember if I didn't want to hire two porters or only one porter was available. Neetu was sleeping on the bench; waking her up, I asked her to go with the porter and instructed her to sit on the luggage in the compartment till I reached. I was already regretting sending the peon back and unaware I had made another blunder by sending a four-year-old child with the porter. In a few minutes the porter was back to take the rest of the luggage. I followed him with Bittu in my arms.

When I entered the coach, Neetu was sitting over the tins of ghee to safeguard the belongings. My breathing came to normal, I hugged my daughter who had shared my responsibility with full vigour. I still get goosebumps when I think of that night. Even if the crime rate was relatively low in those days, the cases of child trafficking and kidnapping were not unheard of. Today if such a situation arises, I would leave the luggage to the honesty of the porter but wouldn't let my children go with a stranger. The best is to travel light.

The city was a witness to two wars

Two wars - 1962 war with China, and 1965 war with Pakistan, marked the decade. Ambala Cantt being the air force station was the centre of action in that region. The wars affected the life of the common man in many ways. There was fear for life and also the fear of shortage of essentials in case the war lasted long. During 1965 war, we lived near Jagadhri Gate in Ambala city. Bittu who was born in 1964 at Police Lines house was seven months old.

After sunset, the entire city would go into blackout. The street lights would be turned off and the lights from the houses too would switch off thus enveloping the entire city into darkness. As the clock struck 5 p.m, the employees would gather their things and leave to be home before the blackout. I would rush home early because the nanny also had to leave. Sometimes on the way I would buy salted boondi (a snack made from chickpea flour) to prepare gravy for the dinner.

At night the dark sky would be dotted with air force planes. Occasionally we would hear of bombs falling on the houses. On government's advice, as a precautionary measure, we had dug a trench which was three feet deep and ten feet long, outside the house; it was meant for three families. At the blaring of the siren, people would rush to their trenches and remain there until the hooting of the siren again, signalling that it was now safe to come out. Many people died of the snake bites in the trenches.

In 1966, we shifted to Model Town. This particular house where we shifted was bombed during the 1962 war and later rebuilt. The neighbouring house was also bombed resulting into the death of a person sleeping in the veranda. That was the only civilian causality in Ambala.

We stayed at Ambala for about ten years, met many good people, and formed new associations. Most of these friendships started as mere acquaintances.

Prof. Ram Yash is one such name that comes to my mind. I met him for the first time in 1951 at the time of first general elections when I had gone to Ambala with mother to address a public rally. He regarded father as his guru, and insisted that we stayed at his house. Prof Ram Yash was a professor of Political Science at Dev Samaj college for girls. He was a philanthropist and so popular amongst the people that the college was referred as Ram Yash's college instead of its actual name. Later, during our stay at Ambala our families became very close. This was the beginning of a life-long association not only with him and his wife Pushp but also with his entire extended family. Ram Yash was like an elder brother to me. He was of immense help when we constructed our house in Ambala, guiding and assisting us on its every aspect. Prof Ram Yash passed away many years ago but I continue to maintain good relations with his wife and other family members.

My friend **Mrs Sudershan Niroola** is another such friendship which started as an acquaintance. We first met in 1962 at some war related function in Ambala. After that we would often run into each other at the war rallies which we both liked to attend. When there was a call to donate for war funds, together we decided to donate a part of our gold jewellery. Her husband Rajkumar Niroola had a high regard for my father and considered me as his sister. We were neighbours in Ambala and later in Chandigarh so we would meet frequently.

Sudershan's jovial nature is her biggest attribute. She turned 90 recently. In spite of many health related issues, she is always cheerful. Her children (Govinda, Rajeev and Mira) and my three daughters became friends, and the friendship continues through the younger generations too.

The list of our good friends is incomplete without the name of **Durga Prashad Singal.** Our association with him goes back to 1957 when Yash ji was a lecturer at Khalsa college in Mandi Dabwali, and Durga Prashad was his student. This teacher-student relationship soon turned into a friendship, and subsequently close family relations. To help Yash ji supplement his income, Durga Prashad would ask his friends to take tuitions from him.

Hailing from a business family, he was not interested in studies but Yash ji motivated him. Consequently he completed his graduation and also the post-graduation in Public Administration. Yash ji started frequenting his house, and the entire Singal family was warm towards him. The family had a humble beginning but with hard work and determination, they flourished and today own multiple businesses in Chandigarh.

Our bond grew stronger when we shifted to Chandigarh. Durga Prashad is like a brother to me. His wife Savita is a wonderful person, always very affectionate and hospitable. When we lived in sector 22, on most Sunday mornings Durga Prashad and Savita would visit us. Sitting in the lawn in our backyard, we would chat over multiple cups of tea, discussing anything and everything from politics to business to families.

There is everything in a name

We were very thoughtful in naming our three daughters. Anita (Neetu) was named after the name of Subhash Chander Bose's daughter. Sujata (Bittu) means a girl with pleasing attributes. There is an interesting story behind Jyotsna's (Guria) name. Before marriage, once I had gone to Chandrawatiganj to attend a training program by Congress Seva Dal. The instructor was a young girl named Jyotsna Sampat. She was graceful and had pleasing manners. I liked her a lot. I thought if I ever have a daughter I would name her Jyotsna which means moonlight. Somehow the names of the elder two were kept by Yash ji but at the time of the third one, I announced the name Jyotsna before anyone could name her.

House number 396, Model Town, Ambala

We lived at this address for four years. This corner house had two portions bifurcated with an imaginary line. Our portion had three big rooms, a living room, a store, and a kitchen. On the other side of the cemented courtyard lived the Nagpal family comprising a middle-aged couple and their four daughters -Saroj, Madhu, Babli and Shashi. The toilet, bathroom and veranda (both rear and front) were common to both the families. We got along well with Nagpals and both families lived like one big family. A few years later we also bought plots opposite to each other's and had planned to build our houses so that we could live together even in our old age but that was not to happen. Nagpals built their house on the plot and lived there until the death of Mrs Nagpal. In 1976 we too built a house on that plot hoping to live there after retirement. The house was given on rent and ultimately sold off in 1995.

In late 1970s, Yash ji was having issues in his job which he would take to his heart and get extremely stressed. Every evening, he would complain of ache on the left side of his chest and we would rush to Dr Sharda Ranjan, the senior consultant at Civil hospital Ambala city. Every time after examining him, Dr Ranjan would assure that his heart was healthy and he could be recommended for the armed forces but in spite of doctor's assurances, the episode of heart ache was repeated every now and then.

In September 1971, Yash ji was selected by Punjab University for the post of lecturer in Hindi at Rohtak. At that time Kurukshetra and Rohtak regional centres were under the umbrella of Punjab University. A notice of three months was required to be given to S.D college in Ambala where he worked but he decided to give only one and a half month notice, and for the remaining notice period he reimbursed the salary. In this way he planned to join at Rohtak on November 18.

After his joining date was confirmed, I rang up the office of the minister in-charge of Public Relations department Mrs Sharda Rani to request her for my transfer to Rohtak. She was not in her office at that time so I gave the message to her PA with a request for my transfer to Rohtak exactly in mid-November, neither before nor later. I didn't feel the need to follow up on this as I was sure that this would be done. As the days of Yash ji's joining date drew nearer, he became tense that I wasn't trying for my transfer.

That day it was a Sunday and I was busy packing his luggage. After five days he had to leave. He was again upset with me as I hadn't yet received my transfer orders. 'I'm not feeling well and you're doing nothing for your transfer. How can you expect a minister to remember the matter when you've not even spoken to her personally,' he whined. Just then there was a knock at the door. The watchman of my office had come to deliver a letter. My face lit up when I read the letter. It was my transfer orders. 'Behenji, this had arrived yesterday but I thought it was nothing urgent and I can give it to you anytime,' the watchman explained. Immediately the packing started. November 18, 1971 was his date of joining in Rohtak. The previous afternoon, he left for Delhi, stayed with his sister Suresh and the following morning took the bus to Rohtak. In the morning of November 18, after sending off our belongings in the truck, I along with our three daughters boarded the bus to Rohtak. I was home by evening and we had our dinner together. I feel in my life, things have always fallen in place on their own without my going out of the way to get them.

Neetu, Bittu and Guria at Model Town house in Ambala in 1970

CHAPTER XV

Punjabis were not welcome in Rohtak (Nov 1971-Feb 1976)

Because of their language and origins, Punjabis were not welcome in the Haryanvi speaking districts. Two of my predecessors at Rohtak Mr A.K Agarwal and Mr Subhash Nirula, both Punjabis, had a tough time during their tenure there. The Haryanvi staff was never kind to them, it was unruly at times and made life hell for them. Mr Agarwal was so distressed with the staff's attitude that he had to remain on three months leave during his stay of about an year, so when the staff at the head office learnt about my request for transfer to Rohtak, they were concerned. Advices and suggestions from well-wishers poured in. Mr Kesari, a freedom fighter and Deputy Director of the department tried his best to make me see the reason. 'Instead you should try to get Gulati ji posted at Punjab University Chandigarh,' he advised but that was not possible immediately. Moreover I was curious to experience the atmosphere at Jat dominated offices and see for myself what kind of people were those who could make life hell for their bosses. Satya Narayan, the stage master whose posting to Rohtak was recommended by me was the only familiar face in my Rohtak office.

In government offices nothing is secret, you say something seriously or casually, it reaches the concerned people even before the words are out of your mouth. Even before my transfer orders were issued, the news of my transfer had already reached the Rohtak staff. The Haryanvi staff was furious at yet another Punjabi joining as their boss. A few retorted, 'we'll see her too. Let her come, we'll send her back packing.' When Satya Narayan heard about such remarks against me, he came thumping his stick on the ground. 'If any of you trouble her even a bit, you see what I do. She is neither Punjabi nor Haryanvi, she is only behenji (sister).' Satya Narayan set the ground for my smooth stay in Rohtak and during my tenure there I got immense respect from my staff.

The overall atmosphere at Rohtak office otherwise too was not cordial. The drama artists would come to me with complaints against each other. I would listen to them but refrain from taking sides. It became their daily routine; the moment I set foot in the office, their complaints would start off. After their show in the village, they stayed there, ate, drank, quarrelled and the next day brought their complaints to me. For a few days I listened patiently but then I told them clearly I was a DPRO and not a judge, they have to sort out their differences on their own. This trick worked. The complaints stopped.

An interesting episode happened during my tenure at Rohtak which is worth mentioning. It was the duty of my department to record the speeches of the chief ministers and send the recorded cassettes to the head office. When Chaudhary Bansi Lal was the CM (from 1968 to 1975), once he addressed an ex-servicemen rally. As per protocol his speech was recorded and the cassette was ready to be sent to the head office in Chandigarh. One evening, at about 5 p.m when most of the staff had left, and I too was gathering my things to leave, CM's son-in-law Captain Gulab Singh came to the office with a friend. He asked me if we had recorded the speech of his father-in-law.

'Yes, we've,' I replied.

He asked me to give the cassette to him.

'Captain Saheb, it can't be given to anybody except our director,' I said flatly.

He was surprised and furious. 'Don't you trust even his children?'

'Not at all Captain Saheb, read the history of old kings and emperors, they all were looted by their sons and sons-in-law.'

My blunt reply left him speechless and he left, his companion followed him. I don't know if he complained against me or not but I didn't receive any communication about it from my director.

After he left, I went to the DC Mr A.N. Mathur and narrated to him the entire episode but he was cool about it.

One of the other colleagues whose memory is vivid in my mind is Mrs Mohinder Nayyar who worked as the publicity supervisor in my department. She was always dressed fashionably in a nice saree, her face bright with make-up. She was older than me by a few years. I was not fond of make-up or even dressing up smartly. In my life, I don't remember using any cosmetics other than Ponds cold cream on my face. I also didn't wear any jewellery - gold, silver or artificial. I always wore simple cotton sarees which were neither stylish nor expensive. I was working in a male dominated field and chose to remain simple, that was my nature and also the demand of my job.

It is worth mentioning here that DPROs deal mainly with menfolk from rural areas so simplicity is always appreciated. Whenever we went out together Mrs Nayyar felt embarrassed because of my simple sarees and plain face. Many times she asked me to dress up nicely and to use make-up or at least use lipstick but I didn't pay any heed to her. When she understood that I wouldn't listen to her, she chose a different route and started instigating my daughters. 'Tell your mummy to use lipstick,' she would prompt my daughters whenever she came home. My daughters too started pressurizing me to apply lipstick at least. I succumbed to the pressure.

Ours was the office cum residence with a door between the two portions. One day a group of four-five elderly Jat men came to the office with a request for sending a drama party to their village. I don't know whether I was looking different or was conscious, I felt when I was talking to them, they were staring at my bright lips. I was embarrassed. The moment they left, I rushed to the bathroom and scrubbed my lipstick off. I returned to my office and called Mrs Nayyar to tell her that I have no problem with her make-up but she was not to instigate my children. She got the message and after that didn't talk about it. We remained good friends till my stay in Rohtak.

1974. Punjab University which was the parent institute for all the regional centres passed an order that the junior most lecturer in Hindi department Rohtak is to be transferred to Kurukshetra with immediate effect as the department in Rohtak was overstaffed whereas Kurukshetra was understaffed. Yash ji being the junior most lecturer was transferred to Kurukshetra. He didn't like Kurukshetra because the living conditions were bad there, mosquitoes abound and the hygiene was poor. Moreover he was given undergraduate classes in the college which was a demotion because in Ambala and Rohtak he had been teaching post-graduate students. He also lacked experience in handling Haryanvi Jat boys who were unruly and attended classes only for fun but there wasn't much of a choice.

By then my father-in-law had relocated to Ambala City after his retirement where they had rented a house near

Jagadhri Gate. Yash ji moved in with his parents and commuted to Kurukshetra every day. He would get up at dawn, have a hurried breakfast, carry his lunch box, catch a local bus to Ambala Cantt station, get on a train to Kurukshetra which was a journey of two hours and return the same evening. Four hours in the day were spent just on commuting. He was not the only one to commute daily, there were many who commuted daily for work.

On his train journey he met the district employment officer, and both became friends. Sometimes when there was no class the following day, he would catch a bus from Kurukshetra to Rohtak and send a word to Beeji through his new friend that he wouldn't be coming home. (In the absence of telephones, the friend had to personally go to the house of Yash ji's parents). Every other day his class would be cancelled and he would land up in Rohtak. On an average, he was in Rohtak for three days a week.

He was disgusted with such a life of catching trains and buses. I applied for my transfer to Ambala so that we could at least be together even if he was not happy with his job. At the same time there were rumours about the bifurcation of Punjab University so I withdrew my transfer application in the hope that Yash ji might get transferred back to Rohtak.

Sometimes in life we feel we are in a terrible situation but that situation is a medium to a better and improved life. Now when I am recalling the incidents from my life, I feel but for this posting in Kurukshetra which he abhorred, we wouldn't have got a chance to live in Chandigarh, the most beautiful city of India. Many good things happened in Chandigarh. Our three daughters got good education there, got married and we made some wonderful friends. I strongly believe that whatever happens in life is for good because God has his own plans.

In 1975 Punjab university was bifurcated into Punjab (Chandigarh) and Haryana (Rohtak and Kurukshetra). Its employees working in Rohtak and Kurukshetra had to remain at their respective places except those employees who were transferred and tormented for no fault of theirs. Such workforce could apply for their transfer to Chandigarh if they wished. Only four people including Yash ji were eligible to apply for the transfer.

His application was instantly accepted and in June 1975 he joined Punjab University Chandigarh. I too applied for my transfer to Chandigarh which was our head office. Transfer to the head office was not easy but two noble persons - Chowdhary Sultan Singh and Chowdhary Ranbir Singh, both freedom fighters, pleaded my case and I was given the coveted posting. With heavy heart, I had to bid goodbye to my colleagues in Rohtak.

My tenure of about five years at Rohtak was extremely comfortable, peaceful and enriching. We loved the city and its people and had decided to build a house there and settle down after retirement but the events changed by the will of God and we relocated to Chandigarh. I was given a very warm send off by my Rohtak staff. A few staff members took charge of the packing and loading the luggage in the truck. (Professional packers and movers were unheard of). Clerk Ahlawat and peon Sher Singh, the hardcore Haryanvi Jats accompanied the truck to Chandigarh, got the luggage unloaded and returned by bus the same evening. These two gentlemen had once opposed my posting at Rohtak. Their gesture touched me.

CHAPTER XVI

Chandigarh - the city beautiful

I joined the Chandigarh office in February 1976. Life at the head office was good but it lacked the excitement of field visits and interaction with rural folks.

I must confess that I am not worldly wise and far sighted. I never thought about the three basic necessities of life - Roti, Kapda and Makaan. In Punjabi these are called Gulli (Food), Julli (Cloth) and Kulli (house). Right from the early days, ours was a double income family and we could've easily owned a big bungalow but because I failed to realize the importance of having our own house, we could buy one only when we were septuagenarians. For me living in a rented house or government accommodation was as good as our own house so why bother about it. During our ten-year stay at Ambala, we changed five to six houses. Locating a new house, packing and shifting every few years was never a bothersome job for me, rather I enjoyed it. So owning a house never came to my mind.

While in Rohtak, I had the dual charge of districts Rohtak and Jind for some time. To fulfil my duties, I had to travel to Jind twice a week. Every time I went to Jind, there would be heaps of applications from the staff for house building loan waiting for my signatures which were later sent to the head office for approval. I wondered why everyone wants to build a house. The common reply was if they didn't build the house during their service it would be almost impossible to do so after retirement. Their words made sense and I too decided to apply for the house building loan. The accountant Mr Bhatia at once typed my application and sent it to me for my signature. The plan was to build our house in Rohtak after the approval of advance but things changed and by the time the loan application was approved, we had shifted to Chandigarh.

It was already March 1976 which was the end of financial year. I was asked to resubmit my loan application in the beginning of the next financial year. My loan would be approved on first come first served basis, I was informed. I reapplied and within a month my loan was approved. I got Rs 58,100 as the house building loan which was to be deducted from my salary in the monthly instalments of Rs 300 until my retirement. We could've built a huge house in Chandigarh with that money but the stars were not in our favour as far as 'our own house' was concerned.

Government accommodation in Chandigarh

On shifting to Chandigarh, we took a house on rent in Sector 19 close to my office. Within a month, I was allotted Type Nine government accommodation in Sector 35. The accommodation was categorized into types depending on the rank of the officers. Type Nine was for senior officers (with basic salary of Rs 550 and above). I took possession of the accommodation but didn't shift there because Sector 35 was not a very well developed area at that time and moreover the flat allotted to me was on 4th floor and had no lift. I gave an application for the change of government accommodation citing that my in-laws were old and couldn't climb the stairs.

In the meanwhile, an officer of the Language department Haryana who was Yash ji's friend and our neighbour requested us to give our allotted flat to a clerk in his office for forty days for performing puja as the clerk lived in a small house and had difficulty performing religious activities. We agreed and gave the key thinking we were doing a pious job. After a month I received a letter from the house allotment committee that I have sublet my flat in Sector 35.

Sub-letting a government accommodation is illegal and the person doing it can be debarred from any government accommodation in future. We were stunned as we hadn't done any such thing. In reality the clerk to whom we gave the key had deceived us. He had sublet our accommodation to four different families who were cooking in all four rooms of the flat. When neighbours got a whiff about it, they complained. With great difficulty we got the flat vacated. In addition to the mental stress that we had to undergo for being naïve, we also had to pay their electricity and water bills as they had left without paying their dues. I sometimes feel that both Yash ji and I easily trusted people. We had to immediately shift to that flat so that we could prove that the complaint against us was false.

Our house owner in sector 19 was a retired Sikh person who was nice to us but neighbours didn't like him. In their opinion he was of quarrelsome nature. The owner's family lived on the ground floor whereas we were on the first floor. A week before vacating the house, we informed the house owner about our exit but didn't give him any more details because of the preconceived notion about him. When our luggage was being loaded in the truck he asked us to tell him at least where we were going. We narrated the entire episode to him. He told us he was a retired superintendent from the house allotment committee itself and could've helped us in getting a house of our choice allotted to us. We regretted not telling him about it earlier but we had to shift out that day as the truck was already loaded. The gentleman was kind enough to plead my case before the committee and vouch for our integrity. I couldn't have sorted out that matter without his help. Later he helped me to get a government accommodation in Sector 22 which was a prime sector. We lived in House number 208 in Sector 22 for 16 years.

As I was already granted the house building loan, we decided to buy a 14 marla plot and construct a house. At that time Mr Mohinder Pratap Mitra who happened to be my tutor in BA was posted as an Estate officer in Chandigarh. He showed us the map of the plots available for auction. We had even earmarked a corner plot for us which was priced at Rs 25,000 but it was not in our destiny.

The evening before the auction, we went to Ramesh Kapila's house where we happened to meet Dr Maini and his wife. Dr Maini was Yash ji's teacher in college and later colleague in the Hindi department. We casually told Dr Maini about the plot auction. The house construction idea didn't go well with him. He discouraged us from constructing a house because we had three daughters and needed money to get them married. He gave logic after logic to convince us that building a house in Chandigarh didn't make a good economic sense which would ultimately take the peace of our family. That was his personal opinion but I got so carried away that I refused to go for the auction the following day.

Because the house loan was already approved , we had to make use of it. The easy way out was to construct a house on our plot in Ambala. We thought Chandigarh and Ambala were so close-by, in future the two cities would be interconnected and we would shift to Ambala after retirement. Soon the construction started on our 600 yard plot in Ambala and within four months a beautiful single-storey house was ready with four large bedrooms, living room, kitchen and front and back yard. In 1976, the total money spent on the construction was Rs one lakh. Immediately upon completion, it was rented out to the malaria department for a monthly rent of Rs 700.

We were living in sector 22 when on April 22, 1980 Beeji passed away at Ambala City at the age of 64. Bauji had been providing honorary medical services at a dispensary run by a philanthropist at Arya Samaj temple on Railway road. He didn't want to leave this service to society but after much persuasion, Yash ji and his brother Surinder who was married and also lived in Chandigarh, were able to convince him to relocate to Chandigarh. Bauji divided his time between ours and Surinder's house in Sector 18. On Dec 7, 1992, he passed away at the age of 86. On Oct 8, 1986, my mother passed away at the age of 83 at Ravi's place at Allahabad.

Me, as a mother

In my own opinion I am just the kind of mother I myself had. My mother had complete trust in me, gave me enough freedom to pursue my dreams, and encouraged me in whatever I wanted to do. Subconsciously I followed her footsteps.

Raising three daughters was neither challenging nor stressful. We were working parents and led busy lives but I trusted them, and was confident that no harm would come to them. If they said they would be late from college because there was an extra class, I never suspected that they might be lying. As a mother, I wasn't authoritative or over protective. Yash ji was very protective towards our girls, he didn't allow them to learn driving whereas I wanted them to learn even flying so there was always a tussle at home. In the afternoons when he would take a nap, they would quietly take out the scooter, and with my knowledge go for a ride. The two-wheeler was kept back before he woke up.

I also didn't impose my aspirations on my daughters, and gave them freedom to pursue their hobbies and dreams. I was financially independent but I never tried to influence my daughters that they must be working women. It was their choice. I was also not worried how would we marry three daughters. I got married without any dowry so I believed they too would find such boys who didn't want dowry. And there wasn't any pressure on them to marry just because they had reached the marriable age. I just let them be and allowed them to live their lives the way they wanted to. I don't know if it's a good parenting. I can't say whether I have been a good mother or not, it is for my daughters to decide.

Neetu, Bittu and Guria are the three precious gems in my life who have always supported me. My daughters have been my strength throughout my life in every sense of the word. They do their best to keep my knowledge updated regarding technology and new age ideas. I learnt using smart phone and even computers from them. I realize when they were little girls I guided them but now in my twilight years, they are holding my hand.

Operation Blue star

In early 1984, military operation was carried out to sniff out the terrorists hidden inside the golden temple Amritsar. Named operation Blue star, this act of government didn't go well with the Sikh community. It intensified the demand for Khalistan resulting into unrest all over Punjab and Chandigarh. The lives of teachers of Hindi and Sanskrit in Punjab were at risk and they received death threats openly. A professor of Sanskrit living in Mohali who had just returned home with his family after performing the marriage of his daughter in Delhi, was shot dead in broad daylight in front of his family members.

There was so much of hatred against Hindus and Hindi that anyone associated with Hindi in any way was targeted. A few days later another professor Dr Tiwari was killed by one of his students. The student visited Dr Tiwari at his house, touched his feet in greeting and shot at him from point blank range. Dr Tiwari collapsed and died on the spot. After these incidents Punjab government provided security guards to those professors of Hindi and Sanskrit who lived outside the university campus.

We lived in Sector 22 and Yash ji too was given 24/7 security. A guard would come in the morning and stay till evening following him everywhere. This took away our privacy. The guard went with Yash ji to the university, and would stand outside the classroom while Yash ji taught inside. Once Yash ji went to Aligarh to take a viva, the guard went with him in the train, all expenses borne by the government. We owned a Pista-green Fiat car (Premier Padmini CH 244), the guard would sit in the front seat next to Yash ji but for those professors who commuted on the two-wheeler it was quite a hassle to take the guard on the pillion. Moreover a guard carrying a big gun and accompanying you everywhere attracted undue attention which was not just odd but also compromised the safety of the concerned person.

At night, a bunch of guards were posted outside our house. They instructed us not to open the door at night even if the doorbell was rung by one of them as there had been instances where the militants would force the guard to get the door opened at gun point. It was difficult to live a normal life under such circumstances. Those times were scary and we sometimes thought of shifting from Chandigarh after our retirements.

In 1992, Punjab University allotted houses within its campus to those professors who needed security and were currently living outside the campus. Yash ji was allotted house number E 52 in the sprawling university campus Sector 14. We lived in that house from the summer of 1992 to the end of 1994 until his retirement. I was retired an year earlier. People advised me to take up a lighter job after retirement but I was done with the work life. I had worked for 34 years and had scaled up from Publicity Supervisor to Joint Director Public Relations Haryana. I now wanted to live an unhurried life.

We visited a fraud guru

Another incident from 1997 is vivid in my memory. Yash ji was a heart patient and was advised open heart surgery. We were obviously worried. Someone recommended us to visit one guru who claimed to have cured many people of fatal illnesses. We didn't believe in gurus but decided to see him anyway. On inquiring we found out that he was currently staying at someone's bungalow in Sector 36. One evening we landed there. His disciples were in hundreds, many of them well-known IAS officers, politicians and even sportspersons. It gave us solace that we were not the only fools to believe in gurus to solve problems.

The guru's durbar was set up in the huge garden, his chair was kept on a small podium in the centre of the garden.

In his absence, his disciples gathered around his chair and pressed its legs as if they were pressing guru's legs. It was a comic scene and many times we wondered why we were even there.

Every evening sumptuous dinner was served to all as langar. First day when we took a thali for the two of us, a stranger joined us and started eating from our thali. We looked around to find out that most people were eating with strangers. Anyone could join anybody and start eating from their thali. Eating from the same thali with strangers didn't appeal to us. We took a roti in our hand and put a little dry vegetable on it and somehow managed to finish. After that we never ate there. At home we had never eaten from anyone's plate or shared glass or spoon even with family members so sharing the plate with complete strangers was disgusting and unhygienic. After that we would just go, sit for some time and come back. One day when we went there, the iron gate was locked and we were informed that guru had left the town. No one heard of that guru again. We anyway were reluctant to meet a guru, we were thankful that he had left.

Our own house. At last

Many years ago the teachers and non-teaching staff of Punjab University had formed a housing society to buy a land and build flats for its staff members. Those who were interested could apply for membership and later buy a flat. Yash ji became a member of the society by paying Rs 50 as the one-time membership fee. In late 80s a large piece of land was allotted for the residential society in Sector 49. The members were asked to deposit 10% of the flat's price (8 lakhs). At that time, the Khalistan movement was at its peak and there was unrest in Punjab and Chandigarh. Peace of Chandigarh was at stake and its future uncertain which resulted into a large number of professors backing out from the scheme. Yash ji and many of his colleagues too didn't pay the initial instalment. Anyway we were not worried as after his retirement we had the option to shift to our own house in Ambala.

It so happened that on the last date Yash ji's colleague Prof Jayaprakash changed his mind and deposited the initial amount for the purchase of the apartment. The next day when Yash ji learnt about it, he felt cheated because all the colleagues had together decided not to go ahead with the purchase of the flats. This remained the reason of grudge between the two throughout their service and even after retirement. Yash ji later repented that he had lost his right to live in that society, so after some time we purchased a flat there from a retired deputy registrar for Rs 12 lakhs in resale – the original price of the flat was Rs 8 lakhs and Rs 4 lakh as the premium. We went to meet Mr Anand, the seller, in his small rented house in Sector 40. He was desperate to sell his flat even without any premium but Yash ji insisted that the prevalent premium of Rs 4 lakhs was his right and must be given to him.

After a few years when that residential society was ready, we were allotted a flat on 2nd floor. It had a big hall, three bedrooms, attached bathrooms, a study, a store, open kitchen, veranda and the full rights of the rooftop. We spent a lot of money to build high quality wardrobes and changed the flooring to pure marble. The flat was on the second floor which was not a problem for us as we were in our early sixties and healthy. We decided to shift from our rented house in Sector 40 (Number 200), to our own flat but again could not do so because of Yash ji's job at

Dainik Bhaskar, a leading Hindi newspaper in Chandigarh. The newspaper's office was located in Sector 25 which was close to Sector 40.

Yash ji worked as an advisor to the editor and loved his job immensely. Having a good job after retirement was a matter of pride and prestige. Moreover, it was also good for his physical and mental health that he remained busy productively. We had to choose between living in our own flat, and his job.

His office timings were from 6 p.m. to 10 p.m. Sometimes the editorials needed to be rewritten and he would return very late only after sending the editorials to the press. Though the official vehicle was provided to him for pick up and drop, we thought it wouldn't be convenient to travel about 20 km to and fro every day in late evening especially in winters when it is freezing cold so in 2005 we gave the newly furnished flat on rent. In 2009, we sold off that flat and bought a house in Sector 38 which was at a walking distance from Dainik Bhaskar's office.

He worked for the esteemed newspaper for about 15 years till the age of 81. He was extremely fortunate to have found a job after retirement which he loved. Sometimes I think he loved his media job more than teaching. House number 836 in sector 38 A is my current residence. On Feb 26, 2018 Yash ji breathed his last in this house at the age of 83.

With mother during one of her visits to Chandigarh - 1982

My three precious gems - at Chandigarh in 1980

Golden years - 50th Anniversary celebrations at Chandigarh in 2009

CHAPTER XVII

Family: My most valuable asset

Elder brother-in-law

Seven years after my marriage, my elder brother-in-law Dr. Bhimsen Gulati married Shirley Beryl Harvey, a very sweet English woman. They got married in Scotland where they lived. They had met in England where he had gone to study FRCS. (He had earlier gone to Canada but later shifted to England) It wasn't a pleasant news for anyone in the family. My father-in-law was vocal about it. He felt, a foreigner wouldn't have the same family values as compared to an Indian girl. However the rest of the family convinced him to accept his son's decision.

In 1966 when the newly married couple visited India, the entire family including my father-in-law gave them a warm welcome. Beeji couldn't pronounce her name so she called her Sheel, and she became Sheel for everyone. Sheel bhabhi was very affectionate and a perfect fit into our close-knit family. She was the epitome of an ideal Indian daughter-in-law committed to her husband and in-laws. Even if she didn't know Hindi and the family especially my in-laws couldn't communicate in English, language never came in the way of our relationship. In early 1970s my brother-in-law joined Indian military service as a captain doctor, and was posted in Pune for three years.

They were keen on settling down in India but couldn't get accustomed to the working conditions in India so they went back to Scotland. The family was overwhelmed by Shirley bhabhi's hospitality in Pune and Scotland. Bhimsen Bhai Sahib passed away on June 25, 2004 in Scotland. After his demise, Shirley bhabhi visited India with their son Arun, to reintroduce him to the Gulati family. Nine months later on March 14, 2005, she too passed away. Their son Arun remains family's only link to the eldest son of Gulati khandaan. Arun is as warm and affectionate as his parents, and maintains cordial relations with everyone in the family. We eagerly look forward to his visits.

My sisters-in-law - Chander, Raj and Suresh

When my marriage was fixed, well-wishers and friends wondered why mother was marrying me (her only daughter) into a family with three unmarried girls. Mother said, 'she always wanted to have a sister, now she is getting three, she should obviously be happy.' As wished by mother, my sisters-in-law - Chander, Raj and Suresh have always been like my sisters and friends. We are still close to each other and I feel free to have a heart-to- heart talk with them. In our younger days we must have disagreed on some matters but I don't remember any incident when we quarrelled or said bitter words to each other.

Chander Kinra, the eldest of three sisters, and younger to Yash ji by four years was considered to be the wisest of all the siblings. No family decision was taken without consulting her, and her views were always unbiased and her suggestions practical. In 1963, she got married to Raj Kumar Kinra, a soft spoken and humble man originally from Pakistan. Raj Kumar was a CA by profession. His father was a freedom fighter like my father so his mother considered me her daughter. Both Raj Kumar and Chander worked extremely hard to give a good life to their children Sanjay and Puneet. Chander started her career as a teacher of Math and rose to become the principal of Raghumal Arya school, Connaught Place Delhi.

From a very young age, Chander was adept in all household chores. She was not only efficient but also swift. She knitted beautiful sweaters for everyone in the family. For Neetu's first winters, she knitted a beautiful red jumper to cover the baby from head to toe. The same jumper was also worn by Bittu and Guria. Chander's best friend Sudesh Bagai who came for the 'girl viewing' in Jalandhar is like family's fourth daughter.

Raj Arora, the second sister is very cool by nature. Being the middle one, she played safe and never entered into any argument. Raj worked as a school teacher. Her husband Kasturi Lal Arora was a lecturer in Jalandhar. He maintained excellent relations with the entire Gulati family throughout his life. We had mutual understanding and faith in each other and could openly discuss any family issue. Raj and Kasturi Lal always remained a voluntary help to our family. Raj now lives with her daughter Seema in Singapore.

Suresh Chugh, the third in the line of sisters, taught Sanskrit in a school in Delhi. Two words that describe her are - gracious host. She got married to Satpal Chugh who was an advocate in Delhi. Suresh and Satpal have been excellent hosts; on many occasions they went out of their way to make others comfortable. In early days, they lived in a small house at 30 Naiwala in Karol Bagh New Delhi in a building where six-seven families resided. Theirs was a two-room set on the first floor, with a tiny kitchen. In contrast to their small house, their heart was big enough to accommodate even a dozen guests.

The Chugh couple was an immense support to us at the time of the marriages of my three daughters. Without their support, we couldn't have performed our duty smoothly. I must also mention about an episode where the family raised their own bar in hospitality. Once on our trip to Delhi , the autorickshaw in which Yash ji and I were travelling, toppled. I was unhurt but Yash ji suffered serious rib injuries. After a couple of days in the hospital, he was discharged but he was not allowed to undertake a five-hour journey to Chandigarh. We had to stay put in Delhi. Suresh and Satpal had shifted to Prasad Nagar by then, they offered their place but their flat was on the second floor. Satpal was gracious enough to offer his aunt's flat on the first floor of the adjoining building who had gone to the US for a few months so we could use one of the rooms.

We stayed in that flat for about a month. For the entire duration of our stay, all our three meals came from Chughs' home. Not just us, Suresh also took care of our guests. Yash ji had a lot of friends in Delhi. Every evening we would have visitors coming over to see him. The moment Suresh knew about the guests, she would arrive with steaming hot tea and elaborate snacks.

Now as I relive those days, I realize it's a herculean physical and financial strain on the hosting family to take care of guests for over a month with so much of love. Even if I want to, I would never be able to reciprocate their love and warmth. Their son Samir has inherited the qualities of his parents.

Devar and Devrani

Kusam , the elder of the two devranis was twenty-five years old when she married my brother-in-law Surinder on Oct 1, 1976 at Ambala. I have yet to see a girl so mature and wise about maintaining relations. She is untouched by anger, arrogance and attitude. Soon she won everyone's hearts and was the most favourite of the family. At the time of their marriage, Surinder was posted in Nabha while Kusam worked in Chandigarh as Employment Officer Punjab. She lived with us. A few months later, I took leave for four months to construct our house in Ambala. Every day I would leave early in the morning. In the evening when I returned, she would've finished all the chores after coming back from office. Now when I think of her as a newly married girl staying with her brother-in-law's family while her husband is posted away, she was not expected to take care of the entire household along with her full-time job. Kusam stayed with us like my daughter, and my three daughters became very close to her especially Bittu, the middle one.

Surinder too has been very affectionate towards my girls. After a few months when Surinder got transferred to Chandigarh, the newly married couple made their own abode and shifted to sector 18 C but they still remained close to heart and not a day passed when we didn't meet. For her 10th exam, Bittu moved in with them to take help from Kusam in Math. In the evening Kusam and Surinder would come home with baby Shalu leaving Bittu at their house to study. Even if we stayed in separate houses we were always one family. In reality Kusam has been and is like my eldest daughter or my younger sister. In 1983, their son Sharad was born.

Col Anil Gulati, the youngest sibling of the family was just a kid at the time of my marriage. At Neetu's birth, he was elated to see a small doll in the house and always wanted to hold her. After coming from school he would throw his bag and run to cuddle Neetu. When Neetu began to talk, Beeji taught her to address Anil as Veera (brother). She couldn't talk properly and instead called him Aila Via. She was very fond of him because of their lesser age difference. Like Neetu, even Bittu and Guria also call him Veera. In 1977, Anil got married to Rita Malhotra. In the initial years of their marriage, when they visited us in Chandigarh, Neetu and Rita would chit-chat all day and roam around in sector 17 like two friends. Anil and Rita are blessed with two daughters – Anureet and Neha.

Sudhir Kant Gupta, my daughters' rakhi brother

Sudhir is my dharam putar (God son) and rakhi brother of my daughters. How and when he became an integral part of our family is coincidental. Neetu always wanted to have a brother. When she was studying in Punjab University Chandigarh, Sudhir was pursuing MBA there, after doing his engineering from Kanpur. She met him in some group, and found him to be a very refined and cultured boy so she and her friends started calling him bhaiya (brother).
In 1983, a day before rakhi, Neetu told me she wished to invite a boy home to tie him rakhi. I was apprehensive, I told her it was easy to make relations but difficult to maintain them but she said he is different and is her brother in real sense. On the rakhi day, Sudhir visited us for

the first time. We felt as if he had always been a part of our family. Sudhir's association with our family started and the bond only strengthened with time.

Not only us but Neetu's in-laws were also fond of him. In July 1984 after Neetu's marriage, her husband went back to USA but Neetu had to be in India as she hadn't yet got her visa. During that one year period, she shuttled between Chandigarh and Delhi where her in-laws lived. Bus was the only means of transport between the two cities. Her father-in-law didn't want her to travel alone so he would always ask Sudhir to accompany Neetu.

At that time Sudhir worked in Delhi. Once Neetu had to come to Chandigarh and Sudhir had an important meeting but as promised, he picked up Neetu from her in-laws' place in Munirka and they went to the bus stand. Neetu asked him to go back to his office after settling her in the bus but Sudhir wasn't up for it. In his view, this was not right and he wouldn't want her father-in-law to lose trust in him. So together they boarded the bus to Chandigarh. After dropping her home, by the same rickshaw he went back to the bus stand to board the bus back to Delhi. This episode speaks a lot about his sincerity and integrity as a human being.

In 2019, when Neetu's husband was sick, Sudhir made a special trip to the US for a fortnight to give her emotional support. I feel relations are not of blood alone. Just by giving a name to a relationship, one is not entitled to rights which come along with it, one needs to earn the respect and faith which Sudhir rightly earned and continues to earn.

The legacy continues...

I am fortunate to have a loving extended family. Not just the first generation but even the second generation including the daughters-in-law and sons-in-law who are now a part of our Gulati khandaan, share the same family values and maintain cordial relations with each other. It takes a lot to build and nurture relations but it doesn't take any effort to break. Forgive, Forget and move on. One needs to start each day as a new beginning - remembering the good things about a person and ignoring the bad is the only way to have good relations.

At 87, I feel the two most valued things in life are good health and strong family bonding. Both can't be taken for granted, and need to be nurtured with patience, love and care.

• • •

With Bhimsen bhai sahib, Shirley bhabhi, their son Arun, my in-laws and our daughters at Rohtak in 1973

• • •

End

Thank You, Dear Mom!

Real life stories are intriguing, more so when your own mother is one of the characters in such stories. Listening to the incidents from her early life in Sargodha, the carnage she and my maternal family endured along with million others – I wonder what gives strength to people to face the tribulations, start afresh and come out stronger. I prodded her to document such incidents. The process that we followed was simple. She would write her memories and share with me to compile, edit and plug the missing links. Some she wrote, and some she narrated, which I transcribed. The fun part of this writing journey was that we could spend a lot of time together - discussing, debating, arguing, disagreeing, and gathering information from relatives whose parents had lived in that era. The outcome is this autobiography which would be cherished by the generations to come with a sense of pride in their lineage.

9 798886 411133

Printed by Libri Plureos GmbH in Hamburg,
Germany